S0-BYJ-517

The Little Giant®

Encyclopedia of

Wedding
Etiquette

The Little Giant®

Encyclopedia of

Wedding Etiquette

Wendy Toliver

A Sterling/Chapelle Book
Sterling Publishing Co., Inc.
New York

Written by: Wendy Toliver
Book Design: Ray Cornia
The author has strived to be as accurate as possible with the exact wording
of direct quotes and with the attribution to original sources listed in the
back of the book. Our apology in advance for any misrepresentation or
inaccuracy due to the reprinting of sources.

Library of Congress Cataloging-in-Publication Data Available

10   9   8   7   6   5   4   3   2   1

Published by Sterling Publishing Co., Inc.,
387 Park Avenue South, New York, NY 10016
Distributed in Canada by Sterling Publishing
c/o Canadian Manda Group, One Atlantic Avenue, Suite 105
Toronto, Ontario, Canada M6K 3E7
Distributed in Great Britain by Chrysalis Books
64 Brewery Road, London N7 9NT, England
Distributed in Australia by Capricorn Link (Australia) Pty. Ltd.
P.O. Box 704, Windsor, NSW 2756, Australia
Printed in China
All Rights Reserved

Sterling ISBN 0-8069-9389-8

Contents

Preface

Whether you decide to simply elope or have an extravagant wedding fit for royalty, deciding to get married is a monumental decision because you will spend a lifetime together as a married couple. As you will soon find out, you don't just marry your fiancé, you also marry the family and gain a whole new circle of friends. Your wedding becomes the event that introduces these people to each other and sets the stage for your future relationships. In this sense, wedding etiquette becomes important in the process of allowing these people to mix and get to know each other in a socially constructive atmosphere.

Married couples throughout the world have discovered that planning the wedding of their dreams can be quite intimidating. If this is your first wedding, or if it has been several years since your last wedding, the process will undoubtedly raise a number of questions. The goal of this little book is to answer those questions for you, equipping you with the answers necessary to accomplish a magical celebration of love—a wedding which can truly be a rewarding and memorable experience for everyone.

The wedding behavior explained herein is grounded in classic etiquette, including the good manners dictated by experts such as Emily Post. However, we have arrived in the twenty-first century, so this classic etiquette is supplemented and sometimes updated to reflect the life-style changes evolution inevitably escorts. Moreover, wedding etiquette varies with each culture, religion, social class, family, and individual. Use the following information as a basic guide, and then subscribe to whatever portions work best for you, as well as the people you choose to involve in the celebration.

This book spells out proper etiquette associated with the wedding, from introducing your intended to your parents, to the wedding day jitters, and beyond. You will also learn where and why wedding traditions originated. This information is intended to give you an idea about why certain rituals are performed in wedding ceremonies. It will further aid you in deciding upon which traditions to embrace for your own ceremony and reception.

Love knows no rule.
— Saint Jerome

Chapter One: The Engagement

Asking their beloved to be their spouse forever comes naturally for some, yet is rather scary for others. Some people get engaged a few short weeks after meeting for the first time, and others are together for many years before the "M" word even comes up. Then when it does, the couple may talk for months before deciding to make a marriage commitment.

Length of Courtship

The length of a courtship has no direct correlation to the success of a marriage. However, a quality courtship—one based on mutual respect and honesty—works wonders in establishing a sound foundation for building a solid, enduring relationship.

Does not act unbecomingly;
It does not seek its own, is not provoked . . .
Love is patient, love is kind, and it is not jealous;
Love does not brag and is not arrogant,
Does not take into account a wrong suffered,
Does not rejoice in unrighteousness,
But rejoices with the truth;
Bears all things, believes all things,
Hopes all things, endures all things.
— Adapted from I Corinthians 13:4–8

Introductions

When the couple's families reside in close proximity to one another, it is probable that they have already met. In fact, the parents might have known their daughter's boyfriend and his family for many years. However, this is not always the case.

Parents

When your parents have never met your significant other, and you are serious and approaching the next step of engagement, you will need to introduce him or her to your parents. This first meeting can be arranged over the phone or by letter. Simply state that you have been seeing each other for quite some time now, and you want them to meet. Then, ask when it would be convenient to get together. The couple should get together with one set of parents, first, followed by a meeting with the second person's parents.

Children

If you have children from a previous relationship, introduce your significant other to the children and gradually include both your children and your significant other in family activities. If your partner has children, the same applies. Do not bring all of the children from both bride and groom together for a formal meeting at this time.

The Big Question

When a man decides to ask his girlfriend to be his wife, he can do so in many ways. Perhaps he takes her on a special date or to a special place, gets down on one knee, recites a romantic speech or poem, and asks for her hand in marriage while dazzling her with a diamond engagement ring. Some fellows choose to ask the question in a very public place, such as flying a banner behind an airplane that reads, "Callie, will you marry me?" Or, someone might arrange to ask privately and, by contrast, romantically.

We loved with a love that was more than a love.
— Edgar Allan Poe

Surprise!

The idea of a man surprising his girlfriend with a marriage proposal is undoubtedly romantic. However, this is getting less popular as many couples prefer to discuss marriage in detail before the actual proposal and engagement happens. Whether the proposal is a surprise or expected, he should put some thought into how he asks her, because she has probably been anticipating this moment for a very long while.

Woman Asking Man

Today, it is rare but truly acceptable for a woman to ask a man to marry her. She will want to do so in a way that does not offend her intended. He need not feel that his masculinity is being threatened; instead, he should feel honored. Since men typically do not wear an engagement ring (they wear a wedding band after the wedding), it is not

necessary for her to present him with one during her proposal. In fact, it is unnecessary for a man to present his girlfriend with an engagement ring at the time of the proposal. However, if a woman asks her boyfriend to be her husband, she can present him with another gift that symbolizes her love and commitment to him, such as a nice watch which has been engraved.

Give all to love; obey thy heart.
— Ralph Waldo Emerson

Length of Engagement

Some people like to be engaged for quite awhile, and others like to get to the wedding as soon after the proposal as possible. An ideal engagement spans at least three months and no longer than a year. This is an appropriate amount of time to plan a wedding, get to know your fiancé's parents and family, and spend time with new and old friends.

I wonder, by my troth, what thou and I did till we loved?

— John Donne

The Ring

When a man proposes to his intended, he usually presents her with a ring. However, having a ring at the time of the proposal is not necessary. Perhaps the couple decides to spend the money on a more pressing issue, like buying a house. Perhaps he wants to save his money longer and therefore be able to afford a nicer ring; or because his fiancée will be wearing it everyday for the rest of her life, he would feel more secure if she helped select the ring of her dreams.

A Welch man used to carve a spoon out of wood and make it into a necklace with a piece of ribbon. He gave this necklace to his intended, and if she wore it, it was a sign that they were "spooning," or engaged to be married.

History of the Engagement Ring

The giving of an engagement, or betrothal, ring is a tradition practiced throughout history in many lands. Prehistoric man tied the wrists and ankles of his bride with grass, believing that this would protect her from evil spirits. The ring being a symbol of marriage might have evolved from an African tradition of tying the bride and groom's wrists together with strands of grass.

In ancient Egypt, rings of precious metals were commonly used as currency, and a husband trustingly placed a ring (his wealth) on his wife's finger. The engagement ring served as a financial payment to a man's future bride in medieval days, as well.

Early Hebrew rings were basic bands of gold or silver, whereas in northern Europe copper, gold, and silver were popular. In the 1800s, jewels and stones began making appearances in European engagement rings. Popular during this time were rings with semiprecious stones and jewels spelling out words like "love" and "forever." During Victorian times, rings plaited from a lover's hair were made.

Simultaneously a symbol of never-ending (thus the circular shape) love and wealth (thus the metal and precious or semiprecious stones), the engagement ring is a sparkling sign that a lady is engaged to be married.

Shopping for the Ring

A ring might be purchased from a reputable commercial jeweler or designed by the couple and crafted by an artist or jeweler. Sometimes, the man has been given an heirloom ring he wants his beloved to wear, but it is generally good decorum to have the setting remade. However, if the ring is in good shape and his intended likes it just the way it is, he can give it to her polished but not altered in any fashion. It is in very poor taste that a man gives his intended the same ring turned down by a former girlfriend, or given to another.

A rule of thumb that many hopeful men follow when purchasing an engagement ring is to spend approximately two to three months' salary. Today, this means the average engagement ring costs between $2000 and $4000. While the woman might want to be involved in the choosing of her own

engagement ring, and therefore be privy to its cost, the ring is still a gift from her future husband. So, the ring should be purchased with the man's money alone.

Diamonds and Other Stones

Most popular is a diamond engagement ring—a custom which historians believe began in the Middle Ages. However, many engagement rings have alternate precious stones set in them, such as rubies, sapphires, or emeralds. A stone can be chosen because of what it signifies; for example, a ruby is for genuine affection and nobility. A sapphire represents everlasting love, sincerity, and truth. The pearl means beauty. Keep in mind that some stones can cost more than a diamond. So do not jump to the conclusion that since a woman's engagement ring has a ruby in it in lieu of a diamond, her fiancé is frugal.

Sometimes, an engagement ring has the couple's birthstones in it. Below find a list of birthstones.

MONTH	BIRTHSTONE
January	Garnet or Zircon
February	Amethyst
March	Aquamarine
April	Diamond
May	Emerald
June	Pearl
July	Ruby
August	Carnelian or Sardonyx
September	Sapphire
October	Moonstone or Opal
November	Topaz
December	Lapis Lazuli or Turquoise

Or, some engagement rings have no stone in them whatsoever. All of these are acceptable, as an engagement ring not only symbolizes love; it also makes a statement about personal taste and fashion.

Love is friendship set on fire.
— Jeremy Taylor

Donning the Ring

A woman can wear her new engagement ring as soon as she receives it—after she accepts the wedding proposal, of course! However, some prefer to wear the ring on the day the official announcement is made, particularly if she wants to surprise her family and friends with the big news.

English women wore wedding rings on their thumbs in the sixteenth century. In some cultures, rings are worn on the right hand, or on any finger and might be switched to the left hand during the wedding ceremony. Jewish brides traditionally wear their ring(s) on the first finger of their left hand. Typically, however, the engagement and wedding rings are worn on the third finger on the left hand, a custom adopted from ancient Egyptians who believed that love made its way to the heart through the vein of this finger called the "vena amoris."

Wedding Bands

The engagement ring may be paired with a wedding band during the ring ceremony of the wedding. If the engagement ring is one of a set, both rings are usually purchased together. While the future bride wears an engagement ring, she does not wear her wedding band until after the ceremony. The future groom does not wear his wedding band until after the ceremony, either.

Oftentimes, the bride and groom choose the wedding bands together. The bands might match exactly, or be of the same metal and styles. Or, they can be entirely different, an independent representation of each person's personality and taste.

Some couples decide to engrave something special on the inside of the wedding bands. If you decide to do this, keep it simple. Ideas include each other's initials and/or the date of the wedding. There is a cartoon that depicts a guy asking another guy if he ever removes his wedding band. In response, he says, "Of course! Every time my wife quizzes me about when our anniversary is!" Engraving the ring is not a common practice, however, and is even considered by some to be bad luck, as it weakens the metal.

I would like to have engraved inside every wedding band "Be kind to one another." This is the Golden Rule of Marriage and the secret of making love last through the years.
— Randolph Ray

Removing the Ring(s)

Taking one's engagement ring or wedding band off was once considered a bad sign—usually that tension or disloyalty brews within the marriage. In the Middle East, to catch a wife who removed her ring to engage in an extramarital affair, her husband gave her a puzzle ring that was next to impossible for her to put back on once removed.

Jewelers recommend removing the ring(s) when sleeping (as the sheets can scratch the ring up over time), cleaning with harsh chemicals, painting, or when doing anything that might harm the ring. In other words, a husband or wife with a bare ring finger is not necessarily a sign that their marriage is in jeopardy.

For years [my wedding ring] has done its job. It has led me not into temptation. It has reminded my husband numerous times at parties that it's time to go home. It has been a source of relief to a dinner companion. It has been a status symbol in the maternity ward.

— Erma Bombeck

A Widow's Wedding Ring

If a widow wishes to wear her wedding ring, it is acceptable. However, if she becomes engaged, she should then remove it and wear the engagement ring given to her by her new fiancé. She can pass her first engagement and wedding rings down to her children if she wishes, or she can have the stone reset into another piece of jewelry.

Behavior Once Engaged

While engaged, it is absolutely inappropriate to take part in dating or sexual activities with anyone other than your fiancé. Being engaged brings with it a code of conduct, which requires complete fidelity and respect to your fiancé, even if you live far apart or have a dispute.

However, you should not become a hermit once engaged. In fact, many couples get so busy with planning the wedding alongside everyday tasks, they barely even talk to one another! With guest lists to prepare; invitations to be selected, printed, and mailed; and locations to be secured, it's a busy time for the engaged couple. This is a very important time in your relationship, and spending quality time together should be made a priority. Go on dates, talk on the phone, send each other love notes and e-mails. Some couples find taking dancing lessons together a fun and worthwhile endeavor—not only do they get to see each other for each class meeting, they learn how to dance— which is beneficial for their wedding reception!

Joy, gentle friends! Joy and fresh days of love accompany your hearts!
— William Shakespeare

The Little Things

Too many times, a person goes through months of courtship pretending to be someone he or she is not. This facade can be very detrimental to any relationship, especially a marriage. Many people get engaged or married and then let their guards down. The husband and wife might stop being polite to one another, stop trying to look nice for one another, and stop doing all the other "little" things that made his or her spouse fall in love during the courtship period. It is a fact that you cannot truly love someone unless you first love yourself. Get to know yourself, and if there are qualities you do not like, make a resolution and take the necessary steps to change for the better.

Marriage is not just spiritual communion, it is also remembering to take out the trash.

— Dr. Joyce Brothers

Discussion Topics

With almost half of all marriages ending in divorce these days, getting to know each other's agendas is vital. Certain topics should be discussed before the wedding to give a couple a fighting chance at a successful marriage. Below are examples of subjects to discuss with your intended before "tying the knot." If there is something particularly important to you, bring it up as soon as possible. Being honest and being able to compromise are invaluable qualities to find in your life-partner and yourself.

• How do you define "love"?
• Are you "in love" with me?
• What are your views about monogamy?

- What are your views about divorce?
- What is your religious or spiritual background, and what do you see as your religious or spiritual future?
- What was your childhood like?
- What was the first thing you noticed about me?
- Do you think we have a future together?
- Do you want to have (or adopt) children, and if so, approximately how many?
- What are your career goals in life?
- Where do you want to live?
- Which of my habits annoy you?
- How much or little time do you see us spending with our parents?
- If you could change something about me, what would that be?
- If you could change something about yourself, what would that be?
- What do our finances look like, now and in the future?

- What are your financial goals? (house, car, boat, land, second house, art?)
- Am I your best friend?
- Do you feel like you can tell me anything?
- What subjects are very touchy with you?
- Do you like my pet?
- How do you want to organize housework?
- What do you hope we are like, as we grow older together?

There are many books, counselors, and other resources available with suggestions about pre-wedding discussion topics—from casual and even silly, to strict and highly serious. Visit your local library or church for more pre-wedding conversation starters.

Grow old along with me! The best is yet to be.
— Robert Browning

Breaking the News

Shout it from the rooftops! You are now engaged!

Telling Parents

By now, hopefully your parents have met your fiancé. And hopefully they like him or her! If you are both without children at this point, it is good etiquette to let your parents be the first to know you are engaged. Traditionally, the couple shares their news with the woman's parents first. It should be done personally—either with a visit from the couple, or if that is impossible, over the phone.

If your or your fiancé's parents are divorced, tell the parent you or your fiancé lives with, or lived with most recently, first. The other parent should be contacted shortly afterward.

In the past, if a young man wanted to marry his sweetheart, he had to first ask her father's permission. Sometimes, he offered the father expensive gifts to prove he could take care of his daughter financially.

Other times, the father showered the future son-in-law with treasures if he endorsed the proposed union. Today, it is generally acceptable for a man to ask a woman to marry him without first asking for the parents' blessings.

If a man has already proposed and she accepted graciously, it is diplomatic for them to meet with her parents together, allowing time for their future son-in-law to discuss his plans with them and address any concerns about his future union with their daughter. Ideally, her parents will be elated and bless the union wholeheartedly. Or, some people feel more comfortable bringing up the news alone with their own parents first, and then bringing in their fiancé later.

Parents Meeting Parents

It is proper for the mother of the groom to contact the bride's parents, expressing her joy and inviting

her parents to meet, especially if they have not made acquaintances with each other up to this point. If the groom's mother (or in the case that his parents are divorced, the parent or guardian he has been living with) does not make the first move, it is fine if the bride's mother makes the call. All that matters in the end is that the parents get to know one another before their children get married.

Writing Letters

In this day, some people consider writing letters a lost art. However, it is perfectly appropriate for the parents of the couple to write a letter to their child's future spouse, welcoming the newest family member. It is also highly commendable for the fiancé's parents to write letters to their future in-laws, complimenting them for raising such a wonderful person and thanking them for welcoming him or her into their family.

Dealing with Disapproval

Occasionally, a parent or set of parents disapproves of their child's choice in a marriage partner. If this is the case, you can either honor your parents' wishes (maybe they have a good point), or go ahead with the wedding despite your parents' feelings. If you chose the latter course of action, be as cordial as possible to your parents. Invite them to the ceremony and let them know it would mean the world to you if they came. Do not, however, expect them to be involved in the planning, financial assistance, or the ceremony itself. If they do involve themselves and offer assistance of any kind, be gracious in your acceptance of their help.

Telling Children

If your fiancé and/or you have children, it is proper to tell them the news about your engagement first. Each parent tells his or her children in the absence of the new fiancé. At this time, allow your children to voice their concerns, happiness, frustration, or whatever they might be feeling. Then, when you feel comfortable, discuss the engagement with your children and your fiancé together. Consistently encourage your children to be honest and open about their feelings.

Telling the Rest of the World

In most instances, formal engagement announcements are not required. Instead, send simple notes or letters, or make phone calls to close friends and family members before your newspaper announcement runs. You will probably be so excited that you will tell everybody—from the mail carrier to the grocery clerk—your big news. Just be certain you notify those closest to you, to eliminate hurt feelings should they find out from somebody else, like the waiter in the coffeehouse down the road.

A Glimpse into the Future

Now that you are engaged, you have several pressing issues to think about, other than planning the wedding itself. Not only are you uniting with this person you love, but also you are uniting two families. You are working toward a successful marriage, after all, and building a strong foundation at this time is of the utmost importance.

Mom? Dad?

The issue about what to call your in-laws can be tricky indeed. On one hand, you do not want to sound overly formal. On the other hand, you do not want to sound disrespectful. Some etiquette experts suggest calling them Mr. and Mrs. White (or whatever their last name happens to be) until they give you permission to call them something else. Of course, by doing this, you might end up calling them Mr. and Mrs. White forever. Some people call their in-laws by their first names. And others use some derivative of "Mother" or "Father."

The best solution is to speak candidly with your future in-laws about what they would like you to call them, and what you feel comfortable calling them. Hopefully, you will come to a compromise and everyone will be happy.

Prenuptials

A prenuptial agreement is a legally binding arrangement made before two people become married. It is usually drawn with the help of an attorney, and the future husband and wife, as well as a witness or notary. A prenuptial agreement is meant to protect one or both individuals should something unfortunate happen to disrupt the marriage, such as death, divorce, an extramarital affair, and so forth.

Drawing up an official prenuptial agreement before getting married is optional, but many couples concur that it is a worthwhile effort—especially when approximately one in every two marriages ends in divorce these days. Moreover, in the event when one person owns many lucrative assets and does not want to risk losing those assets, a prenuptial agreement makes sense. Further, when there are children from a previous relationship who are meant to inherit certain things from their parent, this arrangement can be preserved under a lawful prenuptial agreement. Properly done, a fair prenuptial agreement can resolve many issues.

However, having one's fiancé bring up the matter of a prenuptial agreement is sometimes quite offensive. So if you are interested in making a prenuptial agreement, propose it to your fiancé as soon as possible—and try to do it so as not to offend your intended.

No, Thank You

Marriage? Gulp! Just because you love, like, respect, are attracted to, or enjoy spending time with someone does not necessarily mean the two of you are destined to be husband and wife.

Saying No

"Honesty is the best policy," as the saying goes. You must be honest, both to yourself and to your suitor. The prospect of marriage can stir up dark clouds of anxiety and doubt. If someone has just asked you to marry him (or her), you might feel obligated to say yes so as not to hurt his (or her) feelings. This person cares a great deal about you, and your saying no will undoubtedly be difficult for both of you. However, if you truly care about this individual, and you are not ready to make such a monumental lifelong commitment, you must say so—and the sooner, the better.

Perhaps the time is not right, and you are too young, financially unstable, or intent on building a career. Perhaps you are not really in love with him or her. Perhaps marriage to this person has too many strings attached, or maybe it is for a "wrong" reason—whatever you define that to mean. If you cannot shut your eyes and "see" yourself married to this person for many years down the road, you should say no.

If you always say "No," you will never be married.
— English Proverb

Breaking Off an Engagement

One day, a young man invited his high school sweetheart on a hot-air balloon ride. He wedged out a space between the pilot and another couple, got on his knees, and asked her to marry him. Surprised and embarrassed, the young lady stammered a "yes,"

46

not knowing what to do. After he drove her back home, she shyly admitted to him that she was not ready to get married—and while flattered, she truly needed to say "no." Sure, the young man was hurt, but he appreciated her honesty.

If an engagement is canceled in due time before the wedding, notify those with whom you have shared the news. You can do so by phone or a handwritten note sent in the mail. If a newspaper announcement has already run, a notice should appear in the same paper, stating that you are no longer engaged. No explanation needs to be given in the printed correction.

The woman should return the engagement ring to her ex-fiancé as soon as the engagement is broken. They also return any other substantial gifts they have given each other. Plus, the couple should return any gifts given to them by friends and family for their engagement. If this is too embarrassing to do in person, simply mail the presents back with a note attached similarly worded:

Dear Sue,
Jonathan and I have decided not to get married.
We are returning the lovely champagne flutes.
We appreciate your thoughtfulness and regret any inconvenience to you.

Best Wishes,
Grace

Deceased Fiancé

If your fiancé passes away before the wedding, it is okay if you want to keep the ring(s) and all of the gifts. However, if you feel more comfortable, it is also appropriate for you to send the gifts back to whomever sent them. Additionally, the bride might want to return to his family her heirloom engagement ring or any other gifts holding sentimental value and that they would want to keep in the family.

It is advisable to consider very carefully what relationship you should continue to have with your fiancé's family before making any long term commitments. Hopefully, there will always be a warm and special feeling between you and this family, but you must consider your future and what another fiancé might think of your interaction with these people.

Engagement Party

After the happy couple shares the exciting news of their engagement with friends and family, an engagement party traditionally follows. It is perfectly appropriate to have an engagement party for second marriages, as well. The party can be formal or informal, and it can include just the engaged couple and their parents, or as many guests as the host invites. Everybody invited to the engagement party should be invited to the wedding.

Invitations

Printed invitations, handwritten notes, and phone calls are all appropriate ways to invite the guests to an engagement party. The type of invitation should reflect the tone of the intended engagement party. For example, a formal invitation would not be appropriate for a party to be held at a local pizza parlor.

Here is one way a printed invitation for a more formal engagement party can be worded:

Mr. and Mrs. Scott Thomas
cordially invite you to
The Engagement Party
honoring
Sally Ursula Thomas
and
Kenneth Jay Oswald
Saturday, the thirteenth of January
seven o'clock in the evening
Cherry Hills Country Club

RSVP
Mrs. Scott Thomas
35578 Miners Drive
Platteville, Texas 75663

Below is an example of a printed invitation for a more casual engagement party:

> *Engagement Party*
> *Clam Bake*
> *for*
> *Jordyn and Randall*
> *Saturday, July 5th*
> *8:00 p.m.*
> *Pier 4*

Hosts

Traditionally, the future bride's parents host the party, but it is equally acceptable for the future groom's parents to host it. Or, if the two families live in different cities, it is acceptable for the groom's parents to hold an engagement party where they live after an engagement party has been hosted by the bride's parents where they live. Or, close friends or other relatives can honor the recently engaged with a party. Alternatively, the couple might want to call their friends and family together and surprise them with their big announcement—at their own party.

Toasts

During the party, the guests get to know one another and the couple better, and each side of the family welcomes the new family member. At some point, it is traditional for the future bride's father to propose a toast to the health of the couple. If the bride's father is absent, her mother or another favorite relative of the bride may make the toast. All of the guests, except for the recently engaged couple, stand and then take a sip of their beverages. Next, the groom makes a toast to the bride's parents. Afterward, anyone desiring to propose a toast to the couple may do so.

Gifts and Thank-you Notes

While it is unexpected, some people bring an engagement present. If this happens, open the gifts at a later time, and remember to send a sincere thank-you note. The handwritten thank-you note can be a monogrammed card or a letter written on the bride's personal stationery. The bride should use cards and stationery with her maiden name on them—never her married name (if she indeed takes on the bridegroom's last name) until after the wedding. If someone brings an engagement present at a later time, and delivers it to you personally, it is fine to open the gift right then and thank the person (no need for sending a thank-you note). However, if someone mails a gift or leaves one on the doorstep, open the gift upon receiving it and send a thank-you note as soon as possible.

Newspaper Announcement

Customarily, the parents of the bride put an engagement announcement in their local newspaper. If the parents of the groom live elsewhere, they might ask for a copy of the announcement to run in their local newspaper. The announcement is worded such that the bride's parents are making the announcement, even when appearing in the groom's home newspaper.

The engagement announcement comes out in the newspaper no sooner than the day after the engagement party. Factors that should postpone a public announcement in the newspaper include: either one of the couple still needs to notify close friends and family, either one is still married (no matter how close the divorce is to being finalized), or there is a death or terrible illness in the immediate family of either one. Because a definite date might not be set for the wedding at this point, newspaper announcements can be printed from an entire year up to a mere week before the actual wedding. If at all possible, try to get the announcement submitted so it runs at least three weeks prior to the wedding, with two months prior to the wedding being the ideal standard.

You will need to contact you local newspapers to get a list of their guidelines. Usually, they request that the announcement be sent in a couple of weeks before you want it to appear in the newspaper. The announcement should be typed neatly on standard 8½ by 11-inch white paper. Your name, address, and daytime phone number should appear on the top of each page. You can write the date you wish it to run on the back of the paper on which the announcement is written. If you aim to have it printed in a very predominant newspaper, keep in mind that there are times that there are too many announcements on a given day, and the newspaper must select which ones it can run. Whenever possible, also submit your announcement to a smaller, more localized newspaper.

Reading existing engagement announcements in the paper will give you an idea of what is appropriate. Normally, the below information is included in like order:

- Who is making the announcement (Mr. and Mrs. Mark Wilson)
- Where they are from (of Seattle, Washington)
- Who their daughter is, middle and last name optional (Melody Ann Wilson)
- Who she is engaged to (Mr. Zachary Smith)
- Who his parents are (Dr. and Mrs. Frank Smith)
- Where his parents live (of Spokane, Washington)

- When the wedding is planned (February)
- Where the daughter went to school (University of Colorado)
- Her occupation (Occupational Therapist)
- Where her fiancé went to school (University of Colorado)
- His occupation (Civil Engineer)

Other items of interest that are sometimes written in engagement announcements include parent's social position and occupations, and names of notable family members.

If one of the bride's parents has passed away, the living parent makes the announcement. The fact that her other parent has died is mentioned in a separate sentence. This can be written like: "She is also the daughter of the late Mr. Gregory Jones." If one of the groom's parents is deceased, the words "the late" appear before the name of that parent, and the rest of the announcement remains the same.

If the bride's parents are divorced, are cordial to one another, and equally excited for their daughter, the announcement can be made in both of their names. However, if they are on bad terms, the announcement is made in the name of the bride's mother, typically. If the bride's parents are not a part of her life, the announcement can be written such that their names are not mentioned.

If a bride has been engaged or married before, a newspaper announcement is not necessary. Instead, she can just notify her friends and family with phone calls or notes sent in the mail. However, if she wishes to have a public announcement, this is acceptable, with the bride and groom making the announcement. Most couples submit a black-and-white glossy photograph (again, check with the specific newspaper to determine specific directions) that appears with the text. The photograph can either be of the couple together, which is usually their engagement photograph and can be casual or formal, or it can be of the bride alone.

The Bride's Trousseau

The French word "Trousseau" translates to "bundle" in English. In the past, a mother began collecting precious handmade quilts, clothing, and other personal articles in a hope chest, chest of drawers, or trunk years before her daughter reached an appropriate age for marriage. When the daughter wed, she brought her trousseau to her new home to start a new life with her husband.

Modern Trousseau

Today, a trousseau might take the form of a shopping spree, where a mother buys her daughter personal wardrobe pieces and household items. In a time when you can just go to a store and purchase most of these things (instead of making everything by hand), a trousseau can be put together after the engagement is announced. Because some ladies have been married before, or have been living separate from their parents for awhile, they might not need any new clothes or household items. However, for a younger woman getting married for the first time, a trousseau is a wonderful way to bridge her childhood and her adulthood.

Clothes

The wardrobe pieces should be carefully selected to see the bride through the first season of her married life, but the amount of clothing and lingerie varies with financial limitations, clothing items the bride has already accumulated, and which basics she still needs. If possible, the trousseau includes a wedding dress, going-away ensemble (for after the wedding), and something special to wear on her first night with her new husband (usually a white negligee or nightgown).

Household

Household items such as linen (including bed, bath, and dining table) and kitchenware (including china, stoneware, cookware, service dishes, glasses, and silverware) should also be taken into account when building a trousseau. It is best to start with the basics and then fill in whatever is still needed shortly before or shortly after the wedding. When buying sets of these things, purchase a complete set whenever possible, so as not to be stuck with mix-matched sets should a favorite pattern be scarce or discontinued in the future. Kitchenware items and sets make good wedding or shower gifts, so keep that in mind when registering. See page 143 for more about registering.

Although not traditionally thought of as trousseau items, televisions, stereos, automobiles, recreational equipment, and computers have found their way into the "hope chest" for many brides. These articles can be difficult to afford for some time after marriage, but many people look on them as an important part of "normal" modern life. Collecting them as part of a trousseau is wise.

Chapter Two: Planning the Wedding

Your wedding will surely be one of the most important and memorable events your spouse and you will experience together. From the excitement of finding that perfect wedding gown to the climax of saying "I do" and hearing the same, every detail needs to be carefully orchestrated so the wedding ceremony is one you, your spouse, and your guests will remember fondly forever.

First Things First

You must select a wedding date, and the sooner the better. Things to consider include:

- How long do you want to be engaged before getting married?
- How long do you think it will take to plan the wedding you have in mind?

- What time of year do you want to get married?
- What day of the week do you want to get married?
- Will both your fiancé and you be able to get off work and relinquish any other pressing obligations on the selected date, as well as several days (or weeks) surrounding the date?
- Will the selected date be inconvenient for any of your most important guests, such as parents, grandparents, children, and prospective wedding attendants?
- If you want to have a honeymoon right after the wedding, is that a good time of year to travel to wherever you want to honeymoon?

Involving the Groom

Sometimes, a bride gets carried away planning her wedding and she almost forgets entirely about her groom! While some grooms do not want anything to do with the planning phase, it is good decorum for the bride and her parents to involve him and his parents in the process. The bride need not solicit their approval for each and every little detail, yet involving them in some aspects—especially those involving the groom (like what style of tuxedos the groomsmen and he will wear)—is courteous. The groom and his family should be highly involved in three aspects of the planning—the invitation list, the rehearsal dinner, and the selection of groomsmen and their duties.

Wedding Planner or Coordinator

Some brides decide to hire a wedding planner or wedding coordinator to help plan their weddings. Perhaps the bride and her mother are very busy and cannot take all the time that is necessary to plan the wedding themselves. Or, perhaps you are getting married somewhere unfamiliar and you need help with local services.

While hiring a professional planner will cost some money, sometimes the wedding planner works special deals out with florists, musicians, caterers, bakers, photographers, and reception-site owners, that help keep the amount of money spent overall somewhat reasonable. He or she will work with your budget so that the cost of the wedding is within your means. A wedding planner might charge an hourly rate, or a percentage of the overall cost of the wedding—typically fifteen- to twenty-percent.

Like all people you will be hiring to make your wedding wonderful, you will want to select a wedding planner with a good reputation and who has the same "style" sense that you have. A take-charge personality is essential, yet you want someone who will also listen to your every wish and try his or her hardest to make it a reality.

The wedding planner not only works with respectable and trustworthy service professionals, he or she helps organize the overall wedding so that it flows smoothly from start to finish. Many wedding planners attend the rehearsal and the wedding, so that they can make any necessary adjustments.

The Dream Wedding

Your fiancé and you will want to capture your talents, styles, and dreams to give the celebration your own personal signature. Look all around the world for inspiration, and draw on your experiences together to weave imaginative, meaningful themes and ideas into your wedding. Listen to your mother's and wedding coordinator's suggestions, but the final decision should be yours. However you get there, keep your overall wedding picture in mind.

Formality of the Wedding

There are three main categories for wedding formality: formal, semiformal, and informal. When deciding what type of wedding to have, you will have many considerations.

Formal

A formal wedding typically has at least two hundred guests. The invitations are engraved and formal in appearance. Typically, a formal wedding takes place in the evening. The bride's gown is white or off-white with a train, and she usually wears a veil. There are approximately five to ten bridesmaids, and they wear long, elegant gowns. The groom, groomsmen, and ushers (one for every fifty guests or as many as there are bridesmaids, which stays true for any formality of wedding) wear black tuxedos (top hat optional) if the wedding occurs at or after 5:00 p.m. in the evening. Cutaways and gray

trousers are worn by the groomsmen/ushers in a daytime formal wedding. The ceremony and reception are both held in places with elegant atmospheres (either indoors or outside) with plenty of seating space. An entire dinner is served, and the bridal party and parents are seated at the head table.

Semiformal

Seventy-five to two hundred guests may attend a semiformal wedding. Invitations are engraved. A semiformal wedding can commence in the late morning, afternoon, or early evening. The bride wears a long white or off-white gown, and a train and veil are optional. There are two to six bridesmaids wearing long, knee- or ankle-length dresses. The groom and his attendants wear tuxedos for an evening wedding, and sack coats and trousers or nice suits if the wedding commences before 5:00 p.m. The ceremony and reception are held in nice locations, such as clubs, churches, restaurants, larger homes and gardens, and hotels. At the reception, the guests enjoy a buffet, ranging from gourmet seafood to dainty little sandwiches.

Informal

Less than seventy-five guests come to an informal wedding, and the invitations can be handwritten or even extended via telephone. Never e-mail a wedding invitation! An informal wedding typically takes place in the morning or afternoon. The bride can wear a nice suit, a cocktail dress, or a simple gown—white or another light color for summer or a darker color for winter. There might be no attendants at all, or simply a maid/matron of honor and a best man. Or, there might be just a bridesmaid. The bride's attendants dress similarly to the bride. The groom sports a business suit or a jacket and slacks, as does the best man or groomsmen (if applicable). The wedding site can be in a small place—like a home or a backyard garden—as well as in a chapel, rectory, or courthouse. The reception can also be in a home, church gymnasium, or restaurant. A light meal or snacks are displayed buffet-style.

Master Checklist

To help keep organized, many brides make a master checklist. Every detail of the wedding planning and preparations can be kept in order on a timetable. Below is an example of how you can keep your wedding planning as organized as possible, so that no important details are forgotten or seen to too late to have everything go smoothly.

Six months before the wedding, or as soon as possible:

• Select wedding date and time to begin.

- Decide on how many guests to invite.
- Decide the style of wedding you wish to have.
- Decide what type of reception you wish to have.
- Determine where the ceremony will take place, or at least be looking for a suitable site.
- Determine where the reception will happen, or at least be looking for a suitable site.
- Generate a realistic wedding budget.
- Announce the engagement to friends and family.
- Select an officiant, judge, or whoever will perform the ceremony and schedule meetings.
- Ask special friends and family members to be your attendants.
- Determine what type of music you want and interview musicians.
- Hire a reputable florist.
- Seek and appoint a good photographer.
- Appoint a video cameraperson, if you wish to have the wedding videotaped.

- Research caterers and hire one that impresses you.
- Put together a guest list.
- Select wedding attire for yourselves and attendants.

Three to four months before the wedding:

- Order wedding cake(s).
- Purchase or obtain wedding bands.
- Plan the honeymoon.
- Make final decisions on wedding attire, if you have not already done so.
- Make final decisions on the florist, music, caterer, photographer, and video cameraperson (if applicable), if you have not done so by now.
- Order invitations and announcements.
- Put together a master guest list representing both bride's and groom's families.
- Finalize decisions on ceremony and reception sites.

Two to three months before the wedding:

- Arrange final fittings for bridal gown and bridesmaid's dresses.
- Address, stamp, and stuff invitations.
- Order wedding attire for bride and bridesmaids, and reserve rental clothes and accessories for groom and groomsmen/ushers.
- Finalize specifics with the florist, musicians, caterer, photographer, and video cameraperson.
- Attend meetings and counseling sessions with officiant, if applicable.
- Schedule formal photograph of bride, once she has her gown.
- Shop for any missing trousseau items.
- Register for gifts.
- Begin planning pre-ceremony, post-ceremony, and other transportation needs.

One to two months before the wedding:

- Plan rehearsal dinner.
- Send or phone invitations to rehearsal dinner.
- Begin arranging accommodations for out-of-town attendees.
- Provide musicians with music selection list and/or sheet music.
- Finalize honeymoon trip.
- Finalize all transportation arrangements.
- Host a bridesmaids' brunch or luncheon, if the bride wishes.
- Obtain items such as toast glasses, guest book and pen, cake knife, birdseed.
- Buy gifts for parents, attendants, wedding helpers, and each other.
- Mail invitations.

- Address and stamp announcements (if applicable), and appoint someone to mail them after the wedding.
- Make place cards for reception, if applicable.

Two to three weeks before the wedding:

- Attend to any last-minute details with florist, musicians, caterer, photographer, and video cameraperson.
- Make arrangements for final payments (including tips) for service individuals or companies.
- Confirm lodging arrangements for wedding party.
- Begin packing for honeymoon.
- Confirm number of guests expected for caterer.
- Have all wedding attire and accessories ready to wear.
- Attend rehearsal and rehearsal dinner.

There are some things that you should be doing all along the wedding journey. You and your fiancé will undoubtedly be invited to pre-wedding celebrations, and you obviously need to attend. Additionally, people will start sending presents of all kinds, and you will want to keep an accurate record and write thank-you notes for all wedding gifts and any other gifts for which the bride or groom could not show gratitude to the giver in person. You will also need to refer to your original budget often, and make necessary adjustments whenever necessary. You can juggle the budget around to leave more money for those things you find most important. Lastly, it is a good idea to talk to someone about the wedding day as everything starts coming together. Simply tell this person about the wedding day you are planning as if it was a report or story. This is an effective way to catch problems and glitches you might have initially overlooked.

Types of Ceremonies

There are a plethora of ceremony types to choose from, including: nontraditional, traditional religious, traditional nonreligious, military, commercial chapel services, long-distance, vacation, same-sex, multiple, late-in-life, and remarriage of divorcees. Or, you might chose to elope, in which case the ceremony is minimal.

Creative and Unique

These days, almost anything goes for a wedding ceremony. Some couples exchange vows underwater in scuba gear, deep in a forest under a canopy of trees, on a pair of Harley Davidson® motorcycles, or beneath the goal posts in a football field. A wedding can be light and fun, like a backyard barbeque. Or, a wedding can capture the romance in an old castle or villa. For the adventurous, a hike or rafting expedition make memorable wedding experiences. The couple might choose to draw on cultural ties, getting married in an art museum. The possibilities are endless!

Traditional Religious

If you decide to marry in a church, temple or synagogue, contact its office as soon as you designate a wedding date. You will then set up a series of meetings to plan the ceremony, and certain churches require premarital counseling sessions. While you are undoubtedly busy with getting the other aspects of the wedding underway, keep these meetings a priority. After all, if you want a religious ceremony, the topics you will be discussing in these meetings are the core of the wedding.

It helps to go into the sanctuary and take a good look around. Whether you grew up sitting in this room every single week, or you have never been here before, it will be beneficial to look at it through the eyes of someone about to be married there. Where will you be standing when you say your vows? What color scheme is the room? You might want to choose a color for the bridal attendants' dresses and flowers that does not clash with the colors found in the ceremony room. Where will flowers go? If there is a large window at the front of the room, you will want to consider getting married at a time of day when the guests will not have to squint in the incoming sunlight.

You will want to discuss many things with the rabbi or pastor before the wedding. In all reality, he or she has probably performed numerous weddings and has a pretty good idea what your concerns and questions will be. Do not take everything for granted. These meetings are to discuss your wedding day, and it is important that no surprises await you. Below are some questions that you can ask:

- What are the fees for the use of the church (synagogue, etc.) and its facilities?
- What is the church officiant's fee for performing the ceremony?
- When can I meet with the church's musicians to go over music selections?
- Can secular music be played, or must it all be sacred?
- How much do I pay the church's musicians?
- May an aisle runner be used? Does the church own one?
- How many people can the church hold?
- How should we handle the photography and videography?
- How long is the ceremony, from start to end?
- Where should guests in wheelchairs be seated?

- How many hours before the ceremony can we come in to decorate, if decorating is permitted?
- Can the church's decorative items be moved for the ceremony?
- Are there any requirements for the bridal attire, i.e. long sleeves?
- Will we need to appoint a security guard and/or traffic officer?
- Can rice be thrown outside the building?
- Is there a room where the wedding party can get dressed for the wedding?
- Do you have a copy of your traditional wedding ceremony presentation, and if so, may I read it?
- Can we write and say our own vows?

Some church leaders request that the couple come to a series of counseling sessions before they are wed. These sessions vary in duration and depth with each different religion, how well the leader knows the couple, and the personality of the leader. Popular topics covered include: faith, children, finances, what marriage means, divorce, and any other relationship issue the church leader feels is important to newlyweds. Sometimes, especially if the church leader is from a different generation, he or she will discuss issues that your fiancé and you view as archaic. If that is the case, be as polite as possible. After all, this person is trying to guide you, and he or she has the best of intentions.

Some religious organizations mandate that everybody being married under their roof must be dedicated to their particular faith. So, if the future bride is a member of the church but the future groom is not, this means he must make an important decision. If he decides to convert (perhaps his religion is very similar, so it is not much of a transition), he can do so. If he decides not to join the church, the religious leader might wish to at least familiarize him with the belief system in a series of meetings. Never join a religion—going through a baptism or other symbolic ritual—merely because your fiancé wishes to be married in a specific church. Carelessly going through the motions not only puts you in an uncomfortable position, but it starts your marriage off with a lie. Again, be honest with your fiancé, and hopefully the two of you can come up with a compromise.

Weddings by Religion

Following are certain popular religious weddings briefly described. Keep in mind that these practices are typical but generalized. Even within a particular religion or faith, different wedding practices coexist.

Amish

The Amish wedding is typically held after harvest

and in the middle of the week, so more people can attend. The bride wears a nice dress fit for wearing to church at a later date. Invitations to the wedding are hand-delivered by the bride and groom. The ceremony is simple yet lovely.

Buddhist

The ceremony, usually designed by the bride and groom themselves, is simple and spiritual. Oftentimes, meditation and the burning of ritual incense is a key component. The ceremony is based on Buddhist scriptures, but a Buddhist wedding can take on a Protestant feel. The bride and groom walk down the aisle carrying strands of beads, called juju, which represent Buddha, their families, and one another. A Buddhist monk blesses the union. The bridal couple then shares a cup of sake (rice wine).

Christian Science

Since no minister in the Christian Science church is authorized to perform a wedding, the bridal couple asks a Protestant minister to officiate. Therefore, a Christian Science wedding is quite similar to a traditional Protestant wedding. A Christian Science wedding can occur within the minister's church or at home. No alcohol is served at a Christian Science wedding or reception.

The Church of Jesus Christ of Latter-day Saints (LDS/Mormons)

Members are married either in a religious temple or in a civil ceremony. If both bride and groom have been baptized and meet the special requirements necessary to receive temple recommends from their bishop, they can be married in an LDS temple. When married in a temple, the holy priesthood performs the ceremony, and the couple goes through a series of rituals. While there, the couple is bound together for time and all of eternity, rather than "till death do us part," as with many vows. The bride and groom wear white in the temple. The bride's gown is modest even if elaborate and without a train. She does not wear a veil, and flowers are not allowed within the temple.

If members of the LDS Church do not get married in a temple, a Church bishop can marry them in a civil ceremony. The couple may get married in the temple at a later date, if they so desire—and if they meet the special requirements at that time.

Eastern Orthodox
Eastern Orthodox weddings are similar to Roman Catholic weddings, with variances depending upon cultural customs. Taking place during the day and in the church, the traditional Eastern Orthodox

wedding has two parts. The first part is the Office of Betrothal, which includes the blessing and exchange of the rings. The second part, which occurs immediately afterward, is the Office of the Crowning, when the priest places crowns atop the wedding couple's heads. In Greek cultures, the crowns are made of flora, and in Russian cultures, the crowns are made of metal. The Trinity (Father, Son, and Holy Ghost) is an integral part of the faith, and so many wedding rituals are repeated three times. At the closing of the ceremony, the newly married couple drinks wine from a single cup.

Ecumenical or Interfaith
When the bride and groom come from different religious backgrounds, they might have an Ecumenical wedding. This wedding can be performed in either the bride's or groom's home church, with clergy representatives from either or

both religions performing the ceremony. Organizing the wedding to represent both religions can be a bit difficult, so it is best to openly discuss your wishes with both clergy-members well in advance of the wedding day.

Islam/Muslim

There are so many different customs among the Muslim people. In general, weddings are elaborate and are performed in the Name of Allah. Before the wedding, the bride and groom enjoy dancing, henna painting, and other ceremonies in their homes. The traditional bride dons modest Muslim attire, but in today's more modern culture, some brides may wear attire that takes on a Western flavor. After the wedding ceremony, the bride's parents host a reception party. A couple of days later, the groom's family hosts a reception to honor the bride, welcoming her into the family. The groom's family showers the bride with lavish gifts. In some areas, men and women congregate separately at the wedding and reception.

Judaism

There are three denominations within the Jewish religion: Orthodox, Conservative, and Reform. In Orthodox and Conservative synagogues (which have the strictest guidelines), all men must cover their heads with hats or skullcaps, and the men and women sit on separate sides of the aisle. The rabbi performs the ceremony. The bride walks down the aisle arm-in-arm with her father and her mother. In a Reform ceremony, the bride walks with her father, like traditional Christian weddings.

The Jewish wedding is a celebration embracing both cultural and religious practices. Jews typically do not marry during Passover, and they often marry on

Saturday evening or Sunday so that the Sabbath is left free. The bride partakes in a ritualistic bath, bringing her from a single status to a married status. Jewish weddings oftentimes take place underneath a canopy. During the wedding ceremony, the bride (and oftentimes her mother) circles the groom several times. The Seven Blessings are recited at the end of the ceremony. Another Jewish tradition involves the bride and groom sipping blessed wine from a glass, then the groom covers the glass with a linen napkin and smashes it underfoot while guests cheer, "Mazel tov," wishing the couple good fortune. The traditional Jewish marriage agreement, or *ketubah*, is quite beautiful, and after the wedding couple signs it, they display it in their home for all to see.

Happy marriages begin when we marry the one we love, and they blossom when we love the one we married.

— Sam Levenson

Protestant

Protestant denominations such as Baptists, Episcopalians, Lutherans, Methodists, Presbyterians, and others perform similar wedding ceremonies. These wedding ceremonies vary depending upon denomination, personality of the officiator, cultural traditions, requests from the participants, and even physical characteristics of the facility being used. Though different in some aspects, all Protestant weddings conform to the ideal that uniting a couple in marriage is to be solemnly recognized by both God and man.

A Protestant wedding is a Christian ceremony that takes place in a church, home, or elsewhere. A pastor, preacher, or minister performs the ceremony, depending upon the denomination of the church. Usually, the wedding begins with a processional where the participants follow a flower girl to the alter—or location of the ceremony. The officiator will usually make some comments about the sanctity of marriage and give advice on what the couple should anticipate from this union. The bride is then given to the groom and the congregation is included in sanctioning the marriage. Upon pronouncing the couple married, the officiator may bless the couple and the participants exit the alter.

Rectory

A rectory wedding is held in a clergyperson's study. Basically the religious equivalent to a civil wedding ceremony, a rectory wedding is ideal when religious differences, cohabitation, or the existence of past marriages mar the ability to have a church or synagogue wedding. Or, perhaps the couple wants a religious ceremony, but they want it to be very small and intimate with select family members and closest friends.

The bride does not need to dress up—her "best dress" clothes suffice. However, she may wear a simple wedding gown and a small veil or hat, if she pleases. A groom might wear a suit and tie. Guests (usually only immediate family and a few close friends) wear street clothes, or the type of clothes they normally wear to their church or synagogue.

Typically, a rectory wedding is held in the late morning or early afternoon, and the newlyweds and their guests gather at a restaurant or someone's home for brunch or lunch afterward.

Roman Catholic

Since marriage is a very important part of the Catholic faith, Catholic couples wanting to be married go through extensive premarital counseling before their big day.

Some Catholics do not get married during Lent, and it used to be that a Catholic wedding took place in the morning. However, today, formal Catholic weddings can occur in the evening. A priest performs the ceremony, and ceremonies can last an hour or longer, especially if the Mass is included.

If mass is held during the wedding, the bride and groom kneel on a bench before the altar and receive communion first. Next, the honor attendants and the attendants and the parents of the bride and groom receive communion. Afterward, any guests desiring to participate may do so.

The honor attendants usually stand near the bridal couple, with the other attendants seated in the front rows of the church.

A prayer is usually said to the Blessed Virgin, and the bride and groom place a bouquet on the altar. The priest introduces the newly married couple to the congregation, followed by the recessional.

After the wedding, a reception complete with dancing and alcohol may take place.

Society of Friends (Quakers)

Quaker weddings are usually integrated into a regular Quaker meeting, or they can occur at home. There is no clergy-member officiating the ceremony, and the bride may or may not wear a gown and veil. The couple sits facing the congregation, and the congregation prays and wishes the couple well. Then, the couple stands, holds hands, and shares their vows. No one gives the bride away, for she belongs to herself. A special Quaker marriage certificate is brought before the couple, and they sign it along with everybody present. The certificate is a cherished keepsake, and the newlyweds display it in a prominent place in their home.

Unitarian Universalist

This religion is based on Judeo-Christian beliefs. Each individual in the Unitarian congregation selects beliefs and practices from other religions and philosophies to form their own creed. Some Unitarian weddings are kin to the traditional Christian ceremony, or they can embody any number of rituals derived from other teachings. Because each church is characteristically different, you will want to meet with the officiant to find out which rituals that particular congregation's weddings embody.

Traditional Nonreligious

Some couples do not want a religious wedding ceremony, so they marry in a civil ceremony.

Civil

Typically performed in a city hall, a courthouse, a judge's chambers, or in the home of the justice of the peace, a civil ceremony requires only a marriage license. Today, almost any licensed person can perform a civil wedding. Check with the marriage license bureau to make certain your intended ceremony will be a legal marriage.

Other Types of Weddings

Many types of wedding ceremonies can be either religious or nonreligious, depending upon what the bride and groom desire.

Military

If either or both the bride and groom are members of the armed forces, military regulations should be followed in their wedding ceremony. The groom wears his dress uniform based on several factors. Is his country currently at war, is he off duty or off base, and what is his involvement and rank? Other military-specific factors may dictate the wearing of the uniform. If the groom decides to don his military uniform, any groomsmen/ushers also in the military should wear their uniforms. The wearing of any uniform other than dress uniforms would be inappropriate.

If both the bride and groom are in the service, the bride may elect to wear her military uniform as well. If the groom is not in the military, she should not wear her uniform.

A distinctive custom of the military wedding is the stately arch of sabers or swords the couple walks beneath. The military officers hold their swords up, forming an archway. Sometimes, it is formed at the altar, but usually it is formed outside the church or synagogue. While the military officers do escort the bridesmaids and guests out of the church, the bride and groom are the only people who pass underneath the arch of swords.

Commercial Chapel

For couples not wanting to bother with planning out every detail of their wedding, they might go to a chapel set up for quick, intimate, economical wedding ceremonies. For instance, Las Vegas, Nevada, boasts weddings performed by almost any theme imaginable, or even through a drive-up window! Plus, Las Vegas has built-in entertainment for the honeymoon and the guests alike.

Weekend or Vacation Included

Additionally, some couples decide to have a vacation wedding, where all of the guests share a vacation with the couple. Sometimes, they all go on a cruise or a backpacking adventure. They might all journey to a theme park, ski resort, or dude ranch. As with all weddings, take into consideration the physical and financial limitations of the special people with whom you want to share this wonderful event. After all, great-grandma might not appreciate strapping on rock-climbing gear to see you exchange vows.

Long Distance

Some couples desire to be wed someplace other than their hometown. It may be a tropical paradise, a winter wonderland, or a romantic foreign country. Extra planning is necessary for a long-distance wedding, including transportation. With the assistance of travel agents and the internet, long-distance weddings are becoming increasingly popular.

Same-sex

While homosexual marriages are not legally binding in every state or country, many same-sex couples desire to have a ceremony to profess their commitment to one another. Whether it is legally binding or not (depending on where it is performed), a wedding ceremony uniting two men or two women is similar to a man-woman wedding.

If the decision to marry someone of the same sex is made, the couple already feels very comfortable in a homosexual life-style. In most cases, they are already living together. When they become engaged, hopefully those closest to them already know they are gay, so the news of wanting to marry is the only big news in the engagement announcement. Those who approved of the relationship before the engagement will most likely approve of the upcoming marriage. Sometimes, someone who disapproved before realizes that wanting to marry signifies something stronger and more legitimate than formerly suspected, and he or she might even lead a toast in the couple's honor.

With any wedding—heterosexual or homosexual—there will be someone who disapproves of the marriage. If someone disapproves of the marriage and/or homosexual life-style, all that can be done is to be honest with that individual. Would the ceremony be uncomfortable if that person attended? Would that person be hurt not to be invited, even though he or she has voiced disappointment or disapproval? See page 40 for more about parental disapproval.

The couple might already have someone in mind to perform the ceremony—a friend who is a religious leader, a professor, a spiritual inspiration, or anyone who is, or represents, an important component of their lives. While the proceedings might not be rendered legal, a judge or mayor can still choose to perform the ceremony, if he or she chooses to do so.

If the couple wants to be married in a religious ceremony, many mainstream religious denominations have branches that are gay-friendly. For example, there are various groups that accept gay and lesbian Mormons, a branch of the Society of Friends (Quakers) recognizes same-sex unions, and Dignity U.S.A. is a branch organization of the Roman Catholic Church that accepts gay and lesbian Catholics. There are several other similar organizations, and the church leader of any of these groups will most likely perform some degree of same-sex wedding ceremony without qualms. Also, some mainstream religions give the option of performing same-sex weddings to individual church leaders. For instance, some rabbis, some United Methodist Church ministers, and some Presbyterian clergy will marry a same-sex couple. Religious denominations that are typically willing to perform same-sex weddings include Metropolitan Community Churches (MCC) and Unitarian Universalist.

Alternatively, the couple can bypass the officiant altogether and marry themselves by sharing thoughts, memories, and vows in front of their friends, family, and other acquaintances.

As for the vows, some of the terminology used for a homosexual wedding ceremony differs from that of a heterosexual wedding. For example, an officiant would not say, "husband and wife," "groom and bride," "man and woman," and so forth. Instead, terms like "partner," "soul mate," and "spouse" are used. Also, because homosexual marriages are still controversial for some people, it is appropriate for the officiant's words or the couple's vows to include phrases that encompass the beauty of love between two people, regardless of their sexes. Whether the wording includes anything about being gay is up to the partners.

As for music, select songs that do not play up gender-specific words or traditional man-woman relation-ships. Some gay and lesbian couples choose gay bands and singers to perform during the ceremony and the reception with dual-fold benefits. For one, they are supporting gay musicians and businesses. Secondly, these musicians will undoubtedly have a repertoire with selections suitable for the occasion at hand.

What is worn to the wedding ceremony is up to the couple. You will want to stay true to your personality when deciding. When two men are being married, they generally don tuxedos or suits. When two women are being married, they might both choose to wear dresses, slacks, or any combination thereof.

You
Deep in the heart of me,
Nothing but you!
See through the art of me—
Deep in the heart of me
Find the best part of me,
Changeless and true.
Deep in the heart of me
Nothing but You!
— Ruth Guthrie Harding

Multiple

Sometimes, siblings or very close friends decide to marry in a multiple wedding. The costs of the wedding can be divided with the other couple, unless other arrangements have been made. Because many of the wedding services cost the same whether there is one bride or several, multiple weddings are typically more economical than single weddings.

For the most part, a double (or multiple) wedding is planned like a single wedding. The couples work together to create the wedding of their dreams. The brides will wear similar-style wedding gowns; for one does not want to be wearing an extravagant cathedral-style gown while the other is in a pretty sundress. Likewise, the grooms, groomsmen, and bridesmaids will want to wear similar styles of clothes that complement each other.

Invitations for double (or multiple) weddings can be issued jointly; or, if the brides are not sisters, invitations can be sent separately.

Each couple invites their wedding party, typically the same number of attendants for each couple. Sometimes, the two couples getting married are each other's maid of honor and best man.

The two grooms walk side by side behind the clergy member, followed by one set of the attendants and then the remaining set of the attendants. The first bride's attendants usually separate to the left, and the second bride's to the right. If there are two aisles, the brides walk down their respective aisle at the same time. Or, if there is one aisle, the elder of the two usually walks down first. If the brides are sisters, the father can escort both of his daughters in the processional, one on each of his arms. Or, someone else, such as the mother or brother, can walk a bride down the aisle. The two couples stand in front of the clergy-member, the first bride on the left.

The ceremony for a double (or multiple) wedding should be concise and well organized. Usually, the first couple says their vows, followed by the second couple. Then, the clergy-member pronounces the couples husband and wife (or husbands and wives) together, at the end of the ceremony. The recessional starts with the first couple (the younger bride), then the second couple (the elder bride), the children attendants, the honor attendants, and finally the bridesmaids and groomsmen arm-in-arm.

If the brides are not related, separate receiving lines are more appropriate. The reception for a double (or multiple) wedding is similar to that of a single wedding.

Later-in-life Weddings

When a senior man or woman is spirited and sociable—whether widowed, divorced, or still single—he or she might meet someone special and want to marry. While some cultures frown upon this (notably for widows and widowers), many people are thankful that their loved ones have companionship to share their later years.

Later-in-life weddings can be quaint and simple, or elaborate and rather large. Usually, the wedding occurs without the preliminary hoopla such as showers and bachelor parties. Also, since the couple probably already owns all the material things they want or need at this point, they oftentimes request that gifts not be given, or that a donation be made to a charity in place of a traditional wedding gift.

Remarriage of Divorcees

Sometimes, a couple who previously went through a divorce might make amends, fall in love all over again, and wish to be remarried. Just because they have gone through the ceremony before does not downplay the right they have to celebrate again.

The bride might wear a corsage or carry a bouquet, but she should avoid looking like she did at their first wedding. No one gives the bride away this time, and most remarriage ceremonies omit the processional and recessional.

For a religious ceremony, it might be held in the officiant's study. Or, for a nonreligious ceremony, a judge's chambers work well. Only immediate family (including their children, if applicable) and close friends attend, generally speaking.

When a party or reception is held to honor the remarriage, it should not be as formal as a traditional wedding reception. Additionally, the couple should plan and pay for it in full. Friends and family members are not required to give gifts, but some will choose to do so.

Eloping

Since wedding costs can quickly become more than anticipated, and wedding plans may require many months of planning, some couples choose to elope. This smaller ceremony can take place in a city hall, church, or commercial wedding chapel. Sometimes, the couple goes on a vacation together and returns married. If this will greatly upset your mother, who has been looking forward to your wedding since the day you were born, you will want to break it gently to her, or consider having a small ceremony or reception when you return. Send announcements to friends and relatives after eloping, as they will all want to share your happy news. See page 58 for more about announcements.

The Wedding Budget

A key element in planning the wedding of your dreams is calculating a wedding budget grounded in reality. No one, no matter how skilled in finance or fortune telling, will be able to project a budget that ends up being entirely accurate by the wedding day. Undoubtedly, you will need to make some adjustments to the budget along the way.

If you have an overall total amount of money to spend, you will find that sometimes one thing will cost quite a bit more than you expected, so you must eliminate or somehow shrink the expense of something else.

Below is a general worksheet that can assist the future bride and groom in generating an overall wedding budget:

Budget Worksheet

1. Rings
   (a) One engagement ring
   (b) Two wedding bands

2. Parties and celebrations prior to wedding
   (a) Announcement party
   (b) Luncheons
   (c) Rehearsal dinner

3. Wedding Attire
   (a) Wedding dress
   (b) Veil, jewelry, gloves, garter, and other accessories
   (c) Slip, lingerie, and shoes

(d) Rental fees for groom's formalwear

(e) Rental fees for groom's attendants' accessories

4. Stationery

   (a) Invitations

   (b) Thank-you cards or stationery

   (c) Stamps

   (d) Monogrammed napkins and matchbooks, if desired

5. Gifts

   (a) Gifts for parents

   (b) Host/hostess gifts for pre-wedding parties

   (c) Gifts for all attendants

   (d) Gifts for wedding helpers

   (e) Gifts for each other, bride and groom

6. The Wedding Ceremony

   (a) Site fee

    (b) Officiant fee

    (c) Security fee, if applicable

    (d) Guest book and pen

7. The Reception

    (a) Site fee

    (b) Catering costs

    (c) Alcohol and other beverages

    (d) Toasting glasses for bride and groom

    (e) Linen, equipment, china rentals

    (f) Serving staff fees

    (g) Parking

    (h) Security fee, if applicable

8. Flowers

    (a) Flowers for ceremony site

    (b) Flowers for reception site

    (c) Bouquets for bride and bridesmaids

    (d) Flowers for flower girl, if applicable

(e) Boutonnieres for groom, groomsmen/ushers, fathers, grandfathers, and other special male friends or family members and wedding helpers

(f) Corsages for mothers, grandmothers, and other special female friends or family members and wedding helpers

(g) Other decorations, such as guest book table and wedding cake table

9. Music
   (a) Music for ceremony
   (b) Music or entertainment for reception

10. Photography
    (a) Engagement photograph, if desired
    (b) Bridal photograph
    (c) Ceremony photographs
    (d) Formal wedding-party photographs
    (e) Reception photographs

(f) Candid shots

(g) Wedding album and frames

(h) Extra copies to give as gifts

(i) Videotaping and editing charges, if you wish to have your wedding videotaped

11. Wedding Cakes

(a) Baker's fee

(b) Cake topper

(c) Groom's cake

(d) Knife for cake-cutting ceremony

12. Transportation

(a) Cab fare or limousine rental

(b) Car rental

(c) Airfare

(d) Carriage for photos

13. Honeymoon
    (a) Transportation
    (b) Room and meals
    (c) Entertainment
    (d) Souvenirs and other shopping
    (e) Trousseaux

14. Legalities
    (a) Wedding license
    (b) Lawyer fees for prenuptials, if applicable

15. Contingency fund (for unexpected expenses and any "extras")

Happiness isn't something you experience it's something you remember.

— Oscar Levant

Gratuities for the Wedding Ceremony and Reception

Be certain to read the contracts and double check with all service providers to determine whether or not the tip is included. For example, the caterer might automatically tag a fifteen-percent tip onto the bill. Below find a helpful guide to tipping. Keep in mind that this is merely a list of suggestions, and do not feel obligated to tip any service providers unless they have done a good job. In fact, the service providers marked with an asterisk are to be tipped only if they provide extraordinary service.

Service Personnel Recommended Tips:
*Baker: 5%–20% of bill
Bartender: 20% of bill
*Bridal Planner: 5%–20% of bill
Caterer: 15%–20% of bill
Chauffeur: 15%–20% of vehicle rental cost

Civil Official: Flat fee (however, some judges do not accept money)

*Club, Banquet Hall, or Reception Center Manager: 5%–20% of bill

Coat-check Attendant: $1.00 per guest, or flat fee

*Florist: 5%–20% of bill

*Musicians: 5%–20% of bill

*Photographer: 5%–20% of bill

Religious Clergyperson: Usually in the form of a donation (Ask clergy-member for suggested amount.)

Restroom Attendants: $1.00 per guest, or a flat fee

Valet: $1.00 per guest, or a flat fee

Videotape Cameraperson: 5%–20% of bill

Wait Staff: 20% of bill

As for any other service professionals you hired to help with the wedding, who did an exceptionally wonderful job, a good rule of thumb for tipping is to give them ten- to fifteen-percent of their bill. You can always tip more if their service was out-of-this-world.

Gratuities for the Honeymoon

If you are planning a cruise for your honeymoon, it is wise to read the ship's brochure or look up their web site on the internet because they oftentimes include suggested tipping rates and procedures. A standard way to figure what to tip on your cruise is to take ten-percent of the cost of the cruise, and divide it between those people who tend to your needs while onboard. For example, if you receive above-standard service from the person who cleans your cabin each day, the waitperson, and the buzzer, you divide the ten-percent (total top amount) by three and tip each individual that amount.

If staying in a nice hotel or resort on your honeymoon, your travel agent or the hotel/resort manager can advise you as to the appropriate amount and frequency of tipping there. In general, two dollars a day can be left somewhere in the room, in plain sight, for the person who tidies your room each day. Fifteen- to twenty-percent of your food bill is appropriate for the wait staff or room service. One dollar per bag is customary for a porter, and a few dollars is appropriate for the valet each time he or she brings your car to you. In most cases, if you do not know what to tip someone, stick with ten- to fifteen-percent. This amount is also appropriate in most places around the world.

Another appreciated consideration for service personnel is to give high marks on any service survey cards. Sometimes, raises and/or continued employment are based on survey results.

Who Pays?

Weddings are notorious for costing "a lot of money." One of the biggest stress factors of planning the wedding of your dreams is deciding who pays for what and how to make the event lovely and memorable without exhausting your financial resources. Discussing the issue with your fiancé and parents openly and honestly is *mandatory*.

The following guidelines are intended to give you an idea of how weddings' expenditures are divided; but as with all information in this book, the final decisions need to be based on what is best for both families. A growing trend among weddings is for the groom and his family to contribute equally to the expense of the wedding. In some cases, the groom's family can incur a majority of the expenses. The bride and her family should never ask them to pay for anything other than what is traditional; yet if they offer, it is fine for the bride to accept their generosity. Keep in mind that should the groom and his family be equally involved in hosting the wedding, the invitations should include their names, as well. See page 50 for more on wording the invitations.

Be very sensitive to the financial situations of everyone involved, and never expect to have someone pay for something just because he or she is blessed with a substantial bank account. With divorced parents, second marriages, first marriages later in life, lopsided guest lists, and other such issues, you will want to adapt these suggestions to fit your personal situation. Additionally, some of the following services and wedding props can be gracefully omitted if the budget does not allow for all that was initially considered.

Expenses for the Bride and Her Family

- The engagement party (if they host it)
- The invitations, announcements, enclosure cards, personal stationery, and thank-you notes (including stamps)
- Wedding dress, veil, and accessories
- The trousseau clothing and lingerie
- Their own wedding attire and the attire required by any family members still living at home
- The groom's ring
- A wedding gift for bride and groom
- Bride's wedding gift to groom, if she chooses to give him one
- Attendant gifts
- Bridesmaids' brunch or luncheon, if bride wishes to host one
- Hotel accommodations for bride's out-of-town attendants

- Hotel accommodations and travel expenses for officiant, if officiant is from out-of-town and is appointed by bride's family
- Any bridal planner or secretarial fees
- Rental fees for ceremony site and additional equipment (awnings, carpet for aisle, etc.)
- Fees for all wedding musicians
- The reception
  (a) Rental fee for site
  (b) Food and beverage charges
  (c) Catering charges
  (d) Wedding cake
  (e) Music for reception
  (f) Guest book, wedding register, etc.
  (g) Equipment fees
  (h) Service fees
- The following flowers
  (a) All flowers used to decorate ceremony and reception sites

(b) Bouquets or corsages for bridesmaids, honor attendants, and flower girl(s)

(c) Flowers or corsages for wedding participants in addition to the wedding party and special helpers, friends, or relatives

(d) Flowers sent to any host who entertained in your honor before the wedding

- Bridal photographs, taken before the wedding
- All photographs and videotaping (both formal and candid) of the ceremony and reception
- Transportation charges for the bridal party from ceremony site to reception site
- All expenses involved in parking cars, security, and traffic control

Expenses for the Groom and/or His Family

- Bride's engagement and wedding rings
- A wedding gift for bride and groom
- Gift from groom to bride, if he wishes to give her one

- The marriage license
- Their personal wedding attire and accessories
- Gloves, ties, ascots, etc., for all men in the wedding party (if not included in clothing rental package)
- Hotel accommodations for the out-of-town groomsmen
- Transportation and lodging expenses for groom's parents/family
- Gifts for groom's attendants
- Complete rehearsal dinner
- Ceremony official's fee or donation
- Hotel accommodations and travel expenses for officiant, if officiant is from out-of-town and is appointed by groom's family
- Bride's flowers, including going-away corsages and throwing bouquet
- Groom's and groomsmen's boutonnieres
- Corsages for mothers and grandmothers

- Transportation for groom and best man to ceremony
- Complete honeymoon trip
- In some cultures, the reception hall and/or all liquor served at the reception

Maid/Matron of Honor's and Bridesmaids' Expenses

- Apparel and all accessories
- Transportation to and from wedding
- Bride's gift
- Shower or luncheon for bride
- Individual gift for newlyweds

Best Man's, Groomsmen's and Ushers' Expenses

- Rental of wedding clothes
- Transportation to and from wedding
- Groom's gift

- Bachelor dinner for groom
- Individual gift for newlyweds

Out-of-town Guests' Expenses
- Transportation and lodging expenses
- Gift for newlyweds

Marriage License

The marriage license is the little piece of paper that makes your marriage legally binding. Because requirements for obtaining a marriage license vary greatly from state to state and country to country, and change within those areas quite often, it is important that you contact your local marriage-license clerk before you make any preparations. For example, you might need a blood test, and you might not. You might need to pass a physical examination, and you might not. Also, age of consent varies widely. If either your fiancé or you are a nonresident, different laws might apply. Furthermore, the time lines by which certain tests must be passed, before a license is issued, vary. Again, a simple phone call to your local marriage-license clerk can answer your questions about the process of obtaining this important document.

Sometimes, the bride, groom, and witnesses sign the marriage license during the wedding rehearsal. Or, they may do so during the actual wedding ceremony (perhaps with music playing in the background).

Bridal Registry

Unless the groom objects, he should join his future wife when she registers for gifts. You can register as soon after the engagement as you wish, and since some people refer to the registry for showers and other pre-wedding parties, it might be advantageous to register shortly after the engagement.

Where to Register

You can go to your favorite local department store or specialty stores, many of which are set up for bridal registries. Even home-improvement stores, variety stores, and sporting-goods stores sometimes have bridal registries. These days, you can even register on an on-line store, which is especially convenient for guests who do not live nearby. Also, many department stores are very accommodating for out-of-town guests and will take orders over the phone and make deliveries.

Advantages

Registering helps reduce the problem of receiving duplicate or triplicate gifts, and it also assists guests who do not know what you need and what will go nicely with what you already own. Knowing they are giving gifts you are sure to like is a pleasure and comfort for guests.

Also, sometimes a gift arrives with no gift card, so the bridal couple does not know who sent it. If the gift was one on the registry, the store where the item was purchased can look up who purchased that particular item in their records.

Another benefit for guests is that stores oftentimes offer free wrapping and sometimes free delivery for any wedding gifts purchased using their registry system.

What to Expect

A salesperson (sometimes called a bridal consultant) knowledgeable about the registry system takes the couple around the store and helps them mark their selections, using a worksheet or small hand-held computer. He or she will undoubtedly have suggestions about specific pieces as well as general information about what a couple needs to furnish their new home. If the salesperson shows you a new china pattern that you "just have to have," but you very seldom do any ritzy entertaining, you can select a stoneware set that can be dressed up for those few occasions. A white or cream with a simple, elegant pattern works nicely. If the salesperson shadows you and you would like to make your selections without him or her, kindly ask if you can be left in private. Then, return the worksheet or computer device, ask any lingering questions, and that is it!

Bride's Second Wedding

If this is the bride's second wedding, it is still appropriate to register. However, if friends and family gave you wedding presents for your first wedding, it is proper etiquette to tell them not to give you another gift. This type of polite notification will help guests know what to expect at your wedding and will set them at ease with your expectations and desires.

A simple note like the one below suffices:

Dear Uncle Bert,
I do hope you will be able to come and celebrate our wedding with us. Since this is a second marriage for both of us, we are requesting that gifts not be given.

Your loving niece,
Cassandra

They might still present you with a gift, of course, and you should graciously accept it. The gift registry for a second wedding works nicely if the groom has never been married before, or if the bride and groom have new friends that did not come to her first wedding.

Chapter Three: The Wedding Party

The Selection Process

Selecting your wedding party is a process that requires careful consideration. You want to keep in mind that these people will most likely be greatly honored, yet upon acceptance, will be taking on great responsibilities. When you have determined a wedding date, feel free to begin asking these special people to serve as your attendants. You can ask them in person over lunch, over the phone, or by letter.

Try to strike a healthy balance between asking people you want to ask without hurting anyone's feelings. That is easier said than done, in many circumstances. If you have close family members such as siblings and first cousins, they should be ideal for the positions. However, if the bride has two sisters, both of whom are close, singling one out for the role of maid/matron-of-honor without hurting someone's feelings is tricky business. It is acceptable to have two maids-of-honor, in which case they can split responsibilities and both feel greatly honored. Or, if the groom has three best friends, it is also okay for him not to have an official best man. The three friends would just divide up the responsibilities of best man.

When deciding which friends to invite into your wedding party, think about which have been your friends for a long time, which are currently your most beloved friends, and which will most likely be your friends forever. If someone meets all three criteria, he or she is a good candidate. While it is nice to do so, it is not mandatory to ask someone to be an attendant simply because you were an attendant at his or her wedding. Nor is it mandatory to ask someone from your fiancé's family to be your attendant; however, it is a nice gesture, especially if that person is close to your same age or especially close to the groom.

Life's truest happiness is found in friendships we make along the way.
— unknown

Appointments

Traditionally, the bride appoints all of the female attendants, and the groom chooses all of the male attendants. So, the bride selects the bridesmaids and flower girl(s) and the groom selects the groomsmen, ring bearer(s), and ushers. However, if the bride has a brother, a close male relative, or friend, the groom might ask him to be in his line, and vice versa. Some wedding parties are not divided into men and women. For instance, the bride's male family and friends stand alongside any bridesmaids, and/or the groom's female family and friends stand alongside any groomsmen.

Size of Wedding Party

The number of bridesmaids is typically equal to the number of groomsmen, which balances the wedding party and allows for a more uniform recessional. However, there can be more groomsmen/ushers than bridesmaids, especially if it is a larger scale wedding. The rule of thumb is to have one usher for every fifty guests.

The more formal the wedding, the more people are in the wedding party, generally speaking. On the average, a formal or semiformal wedding party has four to six bridesmaids and at least as many groomsmen/ushers as bridesmaids. Some weddings have no wedding party, some only have the best man and maid/matron of honor, and some have twelve or more bridesmaids and groomsmen.

A friend is one who knows us, but loves us anyway.
— Fr. Jerome Cummings

Maid/Matron (if married) of Honor

The maid of honor is typically the bride's best friend or sister. However, sometimes a bride asks her mother, grandmother, aunt, daughter, or stepdaughter. This individual is someone the bride trusts to help her with everything and anything related to the wedding.

Pre-wedding Responsibilities

• Shop for wedding-related items.
• Help address envelopes for invitations.
• Assist with special events.

- Attend rehearsal, rehearsal dinner, and all showers she's invited to.
- Can throw a bridal shower or bachelorette party, if desired.
- Anything else she can help with.

Wedding Day Responsibilities

- Help the bride dress for the wedding and undress afterward.
- Sign the marriage certificate (if over 18).
- Stand next to the bride and hold her bouquet during the ring ceremony (or any other ceremony where the bride needs both hands available).
- Hold the groom's ring if there is not a ring bearer.
- Adjust the bride's veil and train when appropriate.

- Stand in the receiving line, either to the bride's right or the groom's left.
- Sit at head table if there is formal seating at the reception.
- Make certain the wedding gown and bouquet are taken care of after the reception.
- See that all wedding gifts arrive at a predetermined location, with help from the best man.

Best Man

The best man is usually the groom's best friend or brother. However, he might choose his father, grandfather, son, or stepson. The best man helps the groom with everything and anything relating to the wedding. It should be a man who will know what to do if the wedding cake is stuck in traffic somewhere (heaven forbid), and someone who will enjoy offering the first toast to the happy couple.

Pre-wedding Responsibilities

- Attend all festivities that he is invited to, including rehearsal and rehearsal dinner.
- Buy and give a gift to the groom, with approval and input of groomsmen and ushers.
- Make certain the groom's wedding attire is picked up and ready to wear.
- Organize and hosts the bachelor party.

Wedding Day Responsibilities

- Get the groom to the ceremony site on time.
- Hold the ring to be given to the bride, unless there is a ring bearer.
- Stand next to the groom in the ceremony.
- Escort the maid/matron of honor down the aisle during recessional.
- Make certain the bride and groom are transported to the reception site.
- Sign the marriage certificate (if over 18).

- Help bride's and groom's family distribute checks to service providers.
- Make the first toast to new bride and groom at the reception.
- Make certain the bride and groom are safely delivered to their get-away transportation after the reception.
- Make certain to return the groom's attire if rented, or keep the groom's personally owned attire safe until his return.
- Organize the return of all groomsmen's rented formal wear.
- With maid/matron of honor, see that all wedding gifts safely arrive at predetermined location.

Bridesmaids

Historically speaking, bridesmaids are unmarried ladies, or "maids." Today, however, bridesmaids include women who are married. Bridesmaids are typically female family members and good friends of the bride and/or groom. Girls who are approximately seven to fourteen years old can be junior bridesmaids. They take on as much responsibility as they can handle, and stand next to the bridesmaids during the ceremony.

If a bridesmaid is expecting a baby, and she feels comfortable being a bridesmaid, this is just fine. In the past, a noticeably pregnant lady was deemed unsuitable for the position of bridesmaid, but traditions have evolved. The bride will need to discuss the expectant bridesmaid's needs with her—such as fitting into her bridesmaid dress at the time of the wedding and standing throughout the ceremony—in a personal conversation. It will be important for the photographer to be sensitive when setting up the poses.

Pre-wedding Responsibilities

- Assist bride and maid/matron of honor with pre-wedding errands.
- Throw a bridal shower or party, if desired.
- Attend all festivities they are invited to, including rehearsal and rehearsal dinner.
- Make certain their attire is ready to wear in time for the ceremony.

Wedding Day Responsibilities

- Pick up their bouquets two hours before ceremony.
- Stand next to maid/matron of honor during ceremony.
- Stand in receiving line if asked to do so (next to maid/matron of honor if she is next to the bride, or next to the bride if the maid/matron of honor stands next to the groom).

- Sit at head table if there is formal seating at the reception.
- Assist the maid/matron of honor with any of her duties.

Groomsmen

Groomsmen are usually male family members or good friends of the groom and/or bride.

In the absence of ushers, groomsmen are asked to escort all guests to their seats. A young groomsman (approximately seven to fifteen years old) is called a junior groomsman, and he takes on as much responsibility as he can handle. If there is a junior bridesmaid, he will escort her down the aisle in the recessional. Planning too far ahead for fast-growing children may mean that trouser hems and sleeves need to be adjusted.

Pre-wedding Responsibilities

- Make certain their formal wear is picked up and ready to wear for ceremony.
- Attend all pre-wedding parties they are invited to, including rehearsal and rehearsal dinner.
- Host or help best man with the bachelor party.
- Contribute money and ideas for groom's gift.

Wedding Day Responsibilities

- Arrive early (about one hour) to wedding site to help with last-minute emergencies.
- Escort bridesmaids during processional (unless they precede the bridesmaids) and recessional.
- Make certain all guests have transportation to reception site.
- Help bridesmaids with getting gifts delivered to predetermined location, make certain nothing is left behind at either the ceremony or reception site, etc.

Ushers

The groomsmen can double as ushers, or the groom might choose to honor other special men in his life by asking them to be ushers. There should be one usher for every fifty guests, as a rule. The ushers are typically males.

The usher will ask the guests if they are friends of the bride or the groom, and show them to a seat on the respective side. Friends and family of the bride are seated on the left side, while friends and family of the groom sit on the right side. If the guest is a friend of both the bride and groom, the usher will want to seat the guest on the less-populated side. And if the sides become lopsided, the usher politely asks the guest if he or she minds sitting on the opposite side. Immediate families of the bride and groom should sit on their respective sides.

In a more modern setting, the usher might be instructed to do away with rigid seating protocol and simply seat the guests evenly on each side, regardless of whose friend or relative they are, so that each guest has a unobstructed view of the ceremony.

The usher offers the female guests, and both male and female elderly or frail guests, his right arm while escorting them to their seats. If a female or elderly guest arrives with an escort, the usher traditionally offers his right arm to the lady or elderly guest. The escort follows behind. However, for a modern twist, the usher may walk in front of the couple, who walk arm-in-arm. As he walks the guests to their seats, the usher makes polite conversation with them.

Approximately ten minutes before the ceremony begins, the ushers escort the grandparents down the aisle, if they haven't taken their seats by that time. The groom's mother and father are escorted to their seat five minutes before the ceremony begins, and the bride's mother is taken to her seat last. (If a brother of the bride is an usher, he will want to escort their mother.) When the ceremony commences, at least one usher sits in the back to help latecomers find seats after the processional. When the ceremony is over, the ushers invite guests to exit row by row, starting with the first rows.

Bride's Escort

Customarily, the bride walks down the aisle on her father's right arm, and when the officiant asks, "Who gives this woman to be wed?" he says, "Her mother and I." However, with the multitude of different family situations present today, it is not always feasible for the bride's father to walk her down the aisle at her wedding. Perhaps he is deceased, or he is estranged. In the circumstance that her father cannot escort her, a stepfather, godfather, uncle, grandfather, or older brother are good alternates. Sometimes, a bride's future father-in-law escorts her down the aisle. If her father is not the escort, the alternate does not reply if the officiant asks, "Who giveth this woman?" Instead, her mother (if she is present) says, "I do." In this day, a bride might ask her mother to escort her down the aisle and give her away. This is rarely done, but it is acceptable. Or, a bride might choose to walk down the aisle alone.

Flower Girl(s)

Delightfully unpredictable, flower girls can be assets to your wedding ceremony. Flower girls are typically three to seven years old, and might be younger sisters, cousins, a daughter or stepdaughter, or a special little friend of the bride and/or groom. She wears a dress that looks nice with the bridesmaid's dresses, but in a style becoming to a little girl. She can wear a white or off-white dress, if the bride wishes. A flower girl's parents make certain she is dressed and ready for the ceremony. If her parents are in the wedding party, they should designate someone else to help should she become frightened, bored, or behave inappropriately. At some weddings, the flower girls throw rose petals as they walk up the aisle in the processional. Those who are superstitious believe the petals will make the bride fertile once she steps on them. Or, sometimes, the flower girls hand flowers out to women seated close to the aisles as they walk. The flowers can be carried in a pretty basket or as a bouquet. If you elect to have child attendants in your wedding party, one to three

167

usually works best. Any more might be too difficult to organize.

Ring Bearer(s)

Like a flower girl, the ring bearer is usually three to seven years old. The bride's or groom's younger brother, cousin, son, stepson, or other special youngster can be a ring bearer. He can wear short pants or a miniature version of what the groom wears. The ring bearer's parents are responsible for making certain the boy is ready for the wedding. The ring bearer can escort a flower girl down the aisle, or he can walk alone, in front of the flower girl. He takes the rings, typically tied onto a little pillow with a pretty ribbon, and hands them to the best man or groom for the ring ceremony. If the ring bearer is on the younger side, you might elect to have "fake" rings tied to the pillow and have the best man hold the actual rings for safekeeping. Like the flower girl, the parents or a designated adult must be available should the ring bearer need to sit down or be excused from the ceremony.

Candlelighters

For a formal wedding, the bride and groom can ask two young boys (or girls, or one of each) to light candles just before the mother of the bride is seated. After lighting the designated candles, candlelighters sit next to their parents or another predesignated adult guest.

Train Bearers

If the bride's train is a long cathedral style, two children can help carry it down the aisle in the processional and recessional. They can either sit with their parents or another predesignated adult guest, or stand off to the side when not tending to the bride's train.

Other Honorable Appointments

There are so many things that need to be done to ensure the wedding of your dreams. Some of these tasks can be assigned to paid service personnel. If you know someone special whom you would like to have participate in your wedding, you can ask him or her to perform a duty such as:

- Pass out rice, birdseed packets for departure ceremony.
- Serve refreshments during reception.
- Cut and distribute pieces of cake.
- Oversee gift table, making certain cards of the givers are securely taped on each gift.
- Sit at guest book and greet guests.
- Hand out programs, mass books, or yarmulkes.
- Help decorate ceremony and/or reception sites.
- Sing during ceremony.
- Say a prayer during ceremony.

- Play an instrument during ceremony or reception.
- Read a scripture, poem, song verse, or excerpt during ceremony.
- Offer a special toast during reception.

Chapter Four: Pre-wedding Parties and Celebrations

There are several events and get-togethers that typically take place between the engagement and wedding. These include (but are not limited to): the engagement party, the bridal shower(s), bachelor party, bachelorette party, rehearsal, and rehearsal dinner.

Engagement Party
See page 49 for engagement party etiquette.

Bridal Shower
Historically, when a lady of modest means (and therefore no or little dowry) desired to get married, Her dear friends would come to her rescue, showering her with gifts and items for her trousseau.

Customarily, a bridal shower is given by a female friend or extended family member to honor the future bride. Those who attend a traditional bridal shower are all female; however, the groom might sneak a peek toward the end of the party.

Bridal showers range from formal to casual, usually taking place in a restaurant or a home. In years past, it was unacceptable for the bride's mother, any of her immediate family members, or future mother-in-law, to host a bridal shower. Today, however, shower-givers are often creative. Typically, the maid/matron of honor or a bridesmaid hosts at least one of the showers, and they can host one individually or as a small group.

A bride might have one shower, or many showers. They can include friends, family, or business associates. In the case that someone is invited to

more than one of your showers, let her know that you do not expect her to give you more than one present. It is best not to invite an individual to more than two showers unless she is your mother.

It is perfectly all right to invite someone to your shower who lives too far away to come. The gesture will let her know you are thinking about her and wish she could be there with you. If someone cannot make it to your shower, she might still send a present. However, a present should not be expected simply because she was sent an invitation to the wedding shower.

One event of a shower might be the opening of gifts given by the attendees to the bride (and/or groom). Optional bridal shower events include eating a meal or snack, drinking wine, and playing games. The games usually revolve around themes such as weddings, married life, and the groom. The winners of the games are presented with prizes. Favors are typically given to everybody who attends.

The mother, maid/matron of honor, or another friend of the bride, usually writes down what each person gives the bride. This gives the bride a record of all of the gifts received, which is helpful for writing thank-you notes. If the bride thanks each guest in person at the shower, in addition, she must still write and send a thank-you note.

If a lady has been married previously, it is fine for her to be honored with a bridal shower.

Couple Shower

Couple showers are gaining popularity. The idea behind a couple shower is the same as a bridal shower. The friends, family, and colleagues of the couple shower them with gifts that they will both like. Both the bride and groom are honored, and both men and women are invited.

While a theme of a bridal shower might be "Days of the Week," "Holidays," or "Cooking," themes for a couple shower tend to be more humorous and lighthearted. Common themes for couple showers are "Cocktails/Bar," "Mars vs Venus," and "His and Her Lingerie." (By the way, modeling or trying new lingerie on before the wedding night is considered bad luck.)

Host Gifts

If someone takes the time and spends the money to honor you with a bridal shower (or any pre-wedding affair), it is mandatory to show him or her your sincere appreciation. This can be accomplished by sending the host a thank-you letter or note.

Giving your host a gift is optional, and a host should not expect a gift (besides the thank-you note). If you decide to give your host a gift, it does not need to be expensive or extravagant.

Bring the gift the day of the shower, and give it to your host either before or after the party. In the case that multiple people host an event in your honor, give to each host gifts that are identical or similar in nature. You should include with the gift a thank-you note, which negates the need to mail a thank-you note later.

Love is always bestowed as a gift—freely, willingly, and without expectation. . . . We don't love to be loved; we love to love.

— Leo Buscaglia

Bridesmaids' Brunch or Luncheon

This is an optional event that takes place a few days before the wedding, perhaps on the same day as the bachelor party. Usually, the bride hosts a luncheon for her bridesmaids. The bridesmaids or another girlfriend or favorite aunt can host a brunch or luncheon to honor the bride as well.

The bridesmaids' brunch or luncheon can take place in a restaurant, in a tearoom, at a home, or in a garden. This is an opportune time for the bride to give her attendants their gifts and for the maid/matron of honor to give the bride the gift the other bridesmaids and she jointly bought for her.

May no gift be too small to give, nor too simple to receive, which is wrapped in thoughtfulness and tied with love.

— L.O. Baird

181

Bachelor Dinner

Either the ushers/groomsmen or the father of the groom typically hosts the bachelor's dinner, an optional pre-wedding event. The groom and groomsmen/ushers can exchange any gifts they have for one another at this time. It does not necessarily have to be a dinner. Informal get-togethers and parties are more prevalent than formal sit-down affairs.

Bachelor Party

The bachelor party is a custom that scholars believe started in Sparta. While still very popular, it is an optional event.

Traditionally, the best man organizes the bachelor party, with the input and financial assistance of the groomsmen, ushers, and other male friends of the future groom. Sometimes called a bachelor dinner, it is a celebration typically held in a private room of a restaurant, at a club, or in a home.

Bachelor parties have earned a bad reputation through the years based on the notion that this is the last night a man has to be single, thus he should "live it up." Excessive drinking, strippers, and general craziness are hallmarks of the notorious affair.

Since this book is about etiquette, it must be pointed out that a bachelor party does not excuse any imprudent behavior, no matter how strong the peer pressure or liquor. For example, if the bachelor party takes place the eve before the wedding, the future groom (or groomsmen) should not get so intoxicated that he cannot make it to the wedding. *(Note: It is wise to schedule the bachelor party at least two days preceding the wedding date.)*

Common bachelor party itineraries include: rock concerts, baseball games, boating, fishing trips, camping, skiing, or whatever the groom and his buddies enjoy doing together.

It is customary for the groom to toast his future wife with a glass of champagne at the termination of this evening with his men friends.

Here's to the woman that I love, and here's to the woman that loves me. And here's to all those that love her that I love, and to those that love her that love me.
— popular toast by groom

Bachelorette Party

Tradition has it that the women at the bachelorette party eat a cake with a ring or charm baked into it. She who gets the charm in her piece is going to be the next to marry.

Typically, the maid/matron of honor hosts a bachelorette party, with the aid of the bridesmaids and other close girlfriends of the bride. Like a bachelor party, some affairs tend to get wild, with strippers, alcohol, and mayhem. The bride's girlfriends might take her to a public place and play a game, making her look ridiculous to passersby.

Or, the bachelorette party might be a trip to a casino, the beach, a day spa, or any activity the girlfriends enjoy doing together. Bachelorette parties are rarely the eve before the wedding, as most brides strive for a good night's rest before the big day. Like the bachelor party, the bachelorette party is popular, especially with younger brides, yet entirely optional.

Rehearsal

The rehearsal should be scheduled within five days of the wedding, usually one or two evenings before. The rehearsal should be held where the ceremony will occur, and it lasts two hours or less. By this time, you should have already conferred with your fiancé, your parents, your wedding planner (if you engaged the services of one), attendants, musicians, the photographer and video cameraperson, special speakers, and the person performing the ceremony, so that there are no big surprises at the actual rehearsal. Also, if a wedding program will be used, it is a good idea to distribute a program to each participant.

During the rehearsal, everything is practiced from the processional through the recessional. The musician(s) and passage reader(s) determine what their cues will be. The ushers might wish to practice escorting guests down the aisle, and the rehearsal is an opportune time. (A bridesmaid might act as a guest for them.) The officiant usually takes charge, unless a wedding planner is present. After the rehearsal is finished, everyone should know what to do, when to do it, and what to expect overall.

Sometimes, the bride, groom, and their witnesses (typically the maid of honor and the best man) sign the marriage license and certificate at the rehearsal.

To make things run more smoothly, have only those immediately involved with the ceremony attend the rehearsal. Since the rehearsal dinner usually happens immediately after the rehearsal, those at the rehearsal should dress appropriately for the upcoming dinner.

It is bad luck for the bride to participate in the rehearsal as herself, according to a popular wedding superstition. If you ascribe to this belief, have a friend act as a bride stand-in.

Rehearsal Dinner

The rehearsal dinner is held immediately following the rehearsal. The groom's parents traditionally host the affair. As hosts they stand close to the entryway as guests are arriving and greet them, making introductions whenever necessary. It is also helpful if the hosts indicate where the guests are to be seated.

If the groom's parents live out-of-town, they might ask the bride and her parents to suggest a place to have the rehearsal dinner. Rehearsal dinners range from exquisitely formal at a five-star restaurant to a casual backyard buffet.

If the bride and groom have special announcements or gifts for any of the attendees, this is the perfect time to do so. The rehearsal dinner is also an opportune time to privately pay any fees (or donations) and gratuities to any service professionals who are present.

By the end of the dinner, everyone's questions about the wedding should be answered and each of those involved in the wedding and reception should know his or her responsibilities. As with all events that include alcoholic beverages, transportation should be arranged for people who should not drive themselves home.

Rehearsal Dinner Invitations

A polite phone call or a nicely written note is perfectly appropriate for extending rehearsal dinner invitations. However, many people choose to send a formal invitation via mail, especially when the wedding itself is formal in nature.

Invitations to the rehearsal dinner should be sent three weeks prior to the rehearsal. Make certain to invite the immediate families, people who participated in the rehearsal, out-of-town guests, and the person officiating the ceremony, especially if he or she is a personal friend. Significant others of any or all of those mentioned above should be invited as well. Again, make certain the groom's family and the bride's family invite equal numbers of guests.

Below is an example of how a formal rehearsal dinner invitation might be worded:

Mr. and Mrs. Michael James
Cordially invite you to
The Rehearsal Dinner
Honoring
Amy Jane Watson
and
Jeremy Simon James
Saturday, the second of April
Seven o'clock in the evening
Villa Country Club

A more casual rehearsal dinner's invitation might
read:

Rehearsal Dinner

Honoring

Jennifer and Phillip

Friday, October 9th

8:00 p.m.

Good Days Barbeque Grill

Judy and Michael Strand

RSVP 655-1022

Formal Dining Etiquette

For many people, formal dining is not a normal activity. The wide selection of glasses and tableware can be intimidating, especially when trying to cultivate a positive impression of oneself to the other diners. By understanding some basic concepts of formal dining, anyone can easily fit into the process and enjoy the experience.

The first step in participating in a formal meal is to identify the host(s) and then follow his or her lead. The host is the person who selected the menu and instructed the waiters or waitresses on how the meal should be presented and executed. By following the example set by the host, a person can help fulfill the purpose of the meal and repay the host for his or her kind invitation to the luncheon or dinner.

Seating arrangements are usually a carefully thought-out element for a formal dinner. Some hosts choose to seat people who are acquainted next to each other so they feel comfortable. Other hosts choose to seat strangers next to each other so they might get acquainted. Find out what your host wishes to do and then be supportive.

Once seated, the meal will be served. It is customary for the guests to be served before the host, but the host should signal the start of the meal by taking the first bite. Tradition dictates a good host is to oversee that everyone has been served before beginning the meal. By taking the first bite, the host is checking to see if the food is worthy of his or her guests. The waiters job is to quickly serve the meal and make certain the glasses are filled with the appropriate beverages.

Below is a diagram that outlines the various elements of a formal table setting. While there may be some slight variation to the arrangement for any particular meal, the basic elements should remain fairly constant.

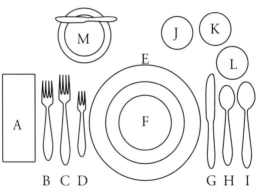

A: *Napkin*

B: *Salad fork*

C: *Dinner fork*

D: *Dessert fork*

E: *Dinner plate*

F: *Soup bowl*

G: *Knife*

H: *Teaspoon*

I: *Soup spoon*

J: *Water glass*

K: *Red wine glass*

L: *White wine glass*

M: *Bread plate*

Occasionally, additional utensils such as dessert spoons, a fish knife and fork, or a crab cracker can be set, but usually they come with the appropriate menu item. Glassware is another issue. It is wise to understand the purpose of each type of glass. If you do not care for a certain type of beverage, it is polite to signal your waiter by turning the glass upside down. Below is a diagram that helps in identifying glassware.

A: *White wine*   E: *Champaign*   I: *Cognac*

B: *Red wine*   F: *Water*   J: *Dessert wine*

C: *Bordeaux*   G: *Cocktail*   K: *Whisky*

D: *Burgundy*   H: *Beer*

Formal dining is an event. The purpose is not to satisfy hunger, but rather to give the guests an enjoyable experience and foster enjoyable conversation. With this in mind, there are several conventions polite guests observe when attending a formal dinner. First of all, politely acknowledge those seated on either side of you and if possible, those seated across the table.

Do not appear to be too anxious to begin eating and thank the waiter for his or her service. While it is not necessary to thank the waiter every time he or she attends to you, it is only good manners to acknowledge their presence when they are near.

As mentioned earlier, do not begin eating until the host or hostess has checked to ensure the food is satisfactory. An old tradition for formal dinners is to never eat everything on your plate. There are many legends as to how this custom began, but probably the most polite explanation is that it demonstrates that your host provided enough food to satisfy his or her guests. When finished with the main course, cross the knife and fork on the plate to signal to the waiter you are done.

Never butter your bread directly from the butter dish. Take a serving of butter and place it on your bread plate. Butter your bread from the butter on your plate. Some people go so far as to only butter the portion of the bread they intend to eat immediately.

At the end of the meal, the host should either thank the guests for enjoying the meal with him (which lets the guests know they are expected to leave), or announce the next group activity. If a guest must excuse himself, this is his opportunity.

Chapter Five: Divorced Parents

Today, a plethora of family circumstances exist. Perhaps one of your parents has passed away, or they are divorced. Maybe your grandparents or another guardian raised you. With stepsiblings and stepparents, single-parent households, and all of the other family arrangements around us, it is no wonder that life can get complicated. If your parents are divorced, you will approach wedding etiquette a little differently than if they are married, especially if they do not get along, or if one or both parents are remarried.

Engagement Party

As for the engagement party, a pre-wedding event typically hosted by the bride's parents, it is important to weigh the feelings of divorced parents. If the groom's parents are divorced, for example, and his mother is remarried to a man his father cannot tolerate, it might be suitable to have two separate engagement parties. Not inviting his mother's new husband is not an option. Another option in a particularly tense situation is to omit the engagement party altogether, and celebrate the engagement in another, less formal, fashion.

Since a family member or a good friend of the wedding couple can host the engagement party, this is oftentimes the easiest route to take when one or both sets of the bridal couple's parents are divorced. Even if the bride's mother is not the official hostess of the engagement party, she and the bride make up the wedding list, preparing theirs and incorporating the groom's and his mother's guest list. They should also invite the divorced father(s) to submit a guest list. Stepfamilies need not be invited unless they are very close with the bride or groom.

If the bride's parents are divorced, yet still friendly toward one another, there is no reason they cannot host the party together. If either is remarried, the stepparents can act as hosts as well, or the stepparents can come as special guests. Whatever the engagement party situation, every host's name should appear on the engagement party invitations.

To follow are some examples of how a more formal engagement party invitation could be worded when divorced parents are in the picture. Because endless host groupings and situations exist, these examples are written such that the parents of the bride are divorced. If the bride's mother is the host, or one of the hosts, of the engagement party, her name (and her husband's, if she is remarried and he is also hosting the party), appears on the first line. Also, the bride's mother's phone number or address is noted for all responses if she is a host. Of course, if the hosts decide to have someone else contacted with the responses, this is perfectly acceptable.

If the bride's parents are divorced yet unmarried, and one parent is going to host the party alone, the invitation would have just that parent's name on it, and any response would be delivered directly to his or her address or phone number.

If the bride's parents are divorced, not remarried, and hosting the party together, a formal engagement party invitation might read:

Mrs. Josephine Simmons Grey
and
Mr. David Gregory Grey
cordially invite you to
An Engagement Party
honoring
Stacy Marie Grey
and
Eric Matthew Bishop
Friday, the nineteenth of March
Seven-thirty in the evening
1228 Main Point Boulevard

If the bride's parents are divorced and one or both are remarried, they might choose to host the party together, with their spouses acting as special guests. In this case, the invitation might read:

Mrs. Mark Hines
and
Mr. Nathan Jasper
invite you to join them
in celebrating the engagement of
Andrea Jasper
and
Craig Smitty
Saturday, the third of August
Five o'clock
Hidden Valley Country Club

If the bride's father is remarried and his new wife and ex-wife all want to host the engagement party, the invitation would be worded similarly to the one previous, except the first two lines would read:

> *Mrs. Elisa Redden Clark*
> *and*
> *Mr. and Mrs. Warren Clark*

or

> *Ms. Elisa Redden Clark*
> *and*
> *Mr. and Mrs. Warren Clark*

If the bride's father and his new wife host the engagement party, the invitation may be worded like:

> *Mr. and Mrs. Stanley Prince*
> *invite you to an*
> *Engagement Party*
> *honoring*
> *Holly Prince and Harvey Kwon*
> *Saturday, February seventh*
> *at six-thirty*
> *The Evergreen Club*

If the bride's mother is remarried, and she and her husband host the party, the first line of the above example would have their names on the top line.

If, by chance, both of the bride's parents are divorced and remarried, and all parents and stepparents host the engagement party together, the invitation might read something like:

> *Mr. and Mrs. Howard James McGee*
> *and*
> *Mr. and Mrs. Tyson Lionel Lambert*
> *cordially invite you to*
> *The Engagement Party*
> *honoring*
> *Candace and Guy*
> *Sunday, September 6th*
> *8:00 p.m.*
> *4877 Highline Crest*

Once the engagement party is underway, tradition calls for a toast to the engaged couple. The father of the bride typically makes the first toast, but her grandfather, stepfather, or other special male friend or relative can take the initiative. The bride's mother, especially if she is the hostess, might also make the first toast to the happy couple. See page 417 for more about toasting at the engagement party. Just make certain the person making the first toast is notified beforehand.

To all the days here and after—may they be filled with fond memories, happiness, and laughter.
— unknown

The Rehearsal Dinner

Customarily, the groom's parents host the rehearsal dinner. If his parents happen to be divorced, their feelings must be taken into consideration. Again, the best way to devise a workable plan is to first have an open discussion about expectations, expenses, thoughts, wishes, and so on. The groom will want to approach his parents to determine what is most comfortable and financially feasible for everyone involved.

The groom's parents who are not remarried and who are on friendly terms certainly might opt to host the dinner together. Similarly, if one or both of his parents are remarried and on friendly terms, they might choose to host the rehearsal dinner together, inviting their spouses as special guests.

If the groom's parents are both remarried, both couples might want to host the dinner. Of course, all four names would appear as hosting the event on the printed rehearsal dinner invitations, if applicable.

If the groom's mother has remarried, and she and her husband wish to host the dinner, the groom's father (and his wife, if he is also remarried) should be invited and seated in a place of honor. The same is applicable for a situation in which the groom's father has remarried.

Furthermore, if one of the groom's parents is remarried and one is not, and they are all cordial to one another, the father, stepmother, and mother can host the dinner.

Of course, the above scenarios are optimistic that the divorced parents are friendly with one another. If they are not friendly, hopefully someone will bow out gracefully. Unfortunately yet realistically, some divorced people simply cannot pretend to be civil in the presence of their ex-spouses.

If the groom's parents are not friendly to one another, it might be easiest for someone else to host the rehearsal dinner. The bride's parents, a favorite relative, or a close friend of the wedding couple might want to take on the responsibility, and this is perfectly acceptable.

Other Pre-wedding parties

As for the pre-wedding parties, such as showers and parties, you will want to consider who you invite, so as not to create any uneasiness. The best way to handle such situations (and most situations) is to be honest and upfront with each parent. There will probably be more than one pre-wedding festivity, so if you need to invite one parent (and his new significant other) to one party and the other (and her new significant other) to the next party, do so. Hopefully, your parents will be so happy for you that they will put their differences aside for a few months and make it a memorable experience for everyone involved.

Wording Changes

You will need to word your newspaper announcement (see page 58) and wedding invitations (see page 60) a little differently, if your parents are divorced.

Financial Aspects

The predicament of financial contributions is a little muddier with divorced parents, whether they get along with each other, or not. The best approach is to speak openly with your parents (and their significant others, if applicable) separately, and ascertain what they feel comfortable paying for. They might offer a lump sum, or mention a certain part of the wedding (i.e. the reception) that they desire to sponsor.

On pages 137–142 you will find a budget worksheet that indicates who traditionally pays for what in a wedding. If any of the wedding couple's parents are divorced, you can put "Mother" and "Father" beside each item and after open discussion with each divorced parent, check which one will pay for each item or service. For instance, if the bride's parents are divorced and her father wants to pay for the wedding cake, she would check "Father" beside that item on her budget worksheet.

The topic of paying for a wedding is a sensitive one in any case. If you find that dividing up the expenses (if your parents agree to contribute financially) is too confusing or causing too much tension between divorced parents, a wedding planner or coordinator can act as a mediator for all parties involved.

If a parent (or both parents) does not want to or is unable to contribute financially, this might be discouraging for you. Hide your anger or disappointment and remember the best gifts a parent can give you on your wedding day are their presence, well wishes, and love.

Chapter Six: Guests and Invitations

Wedding invitations should be sent four to six weeks prior to the ceremony. Therefore, they should be ordered shortly after the date is determined, the locations of the ceremony and reception are booked, and the list is prepared. Sometimes, stationers will agree to give you the envelopes upon ordering, so you can begin addressing them in advance. Be certain to order several extra envelopes (approximately 10% more), in case a mistake is made while addressing them.

If the wedding is very informal, invitations can be sent or issued by telephone up to ten days before the wedding date. If the wedding is formal, engraved invitations are in order.

The invitation itself gives the prospective guests a preview of the formality and style of the wedding, so you should take special consideration to ensure consistency. For instance, a formal wedding will have a formal invitation and an informal wedding's invitation will be more casual in appearance and tone. A creative wedding should have unique and state-of-the-art invitations; and a smaller, friendly wedding can have poetic invitations written by the bride or groom.

Who to Invite

Soon after you become engaged, begin jotting down names of guests you want to invite to the wedding. Part of the excitement is whose faces you imagine beaming up at you as you say, "I do."

A wedding guest list is made up of four sub-lists:

    1. Bride
    2. Groom

3. Bride's parents
4. Groom's parents

Oftentimes, names on the sub-lists are in duplicate. For example, both the bride and her parents will want to invite Uncle Harry. And both the groom and the bride will want to invite Jennifer Brown, their friend from college.

Guests from Both Sides

The bride's mother is in charge of contacting the groom's mother and letting her know the number of guests each family can invite. The groom's family should try and stay within the set limit, but if they simply cannot do so, they can offer to pay the expenses for the extra guests. The number of guests each family invites should be as equal as possible except in circumstances such as the groom being from another city.

Finding Balance

Many newlyweds lament about not recognizing anybody at their wedding, because their parents got carried away inviting all of their friends. In weddings paid and/or planned primarily by the bride's parents and/or the groom's parents, it is easy to see how this happens. Finding a healthy balance between your parents' friends and your friends at your wedding is tricky business. If you need to discuss this issue with your parents, keep in mind that they are extremely excited for you, and they just want everybody to be there. If their addendums to your invitation list make your wedding balloon to the point of explosion, try to create an effective compromise. Insist on sticking to a comfortable number that fits both space and budget. There will always be somebody you wish you could have invited, but the line must be drawn somewhere.

Organized, Neat, and Accurate

While compiling the guest list, try to do so as organized as humanly possible. Some wedding experts suggest writing each guest (and partner/family)'s name(s) and address on an individual index card. Other information to put on each card includes: what gift was given and if a thank-you note has been written, menu selections and seating assignments for the receptions, etc. The cards can be organized into files (or piles) divided into specific categories, for further organization. One such category would be whether the invitee is a guest of the bride and her family, or the groom and his family. The cards can be divided into "Bride" and "Groom." Further, if Mark and Mary Montgomery are friends of the groom, but they live in Norway and probably cannot make the trip to Hawaii, you can place their index card in a file categorized as "Need to be invited, but probably cannot come." Then, after you begin receiving replies, you can file the index cards into different folders for "Yes, we're coming," and "No, we can't make it." Of course, this is just a suggestion and whatever you do to keep it all organized so that no one is forgotten is up to you.

When discussing the guest list with everyone who is involved, stress the importance of correct spellings for the names and addresses being submitted. A quick phone call or looking up the information on the internet or in the phone book while the list is being generated is much more effective than waiting until the envelopes are being addressed later on. Oftentimes, the bride does not personally know everyone invited to her wedding, and she has no way of knowing whether the names and addresses are accurate. Also, a typed list is favored over a handwritten list, as sometimes other people's handwriting is difficult to decipher.

Guest Levels

Traditionally, there are five levels of invitees. These levels can help you decide what size of wedding to have, and where to draw the line, if need be.

Level A: Immediate Family (Parents, Siblings, Grandparents)

Level B: Extended Family (Aunts, Uncles, Cousins)

Level C: Friends of the Bridal Couple

Level D: Friends of Family

Level E: Parents and Bridal Couple's Associates

Double the Guests

If you invite someone who is engaged or married, it is necessary to invite his or her significant other. This is true even if you have never met the other person. Likewise, if you invite a single adult (eighteen years or older), it is polite to add "and guest" to the invitation. Most adults who come to your wedding will be paired with someone else, thereby doubling your guest list.

Out-of-town Guests

If a friend or family member lives a great distance away, or you know he or she cannot attend due to financial restraints or a former obligation, should you send an invitation? This depends on the person. You might elect to send an invitation regardless, knowing that the person would be disappointed to receive only an announcement. Keep in mind that whomever you send an invitation will feel obligated to send a gift. An announcement, on the other hand, does not mandate a wedding gift.

Accommodations

When guests have to travel great distances to attend your wedding, you should make it as easy for them as possible. Send accommodation information to them in plenty of time for them to make arrangements (approximately six to eight weeks). If you endorse a particular hotel, motel, or bed and breakfast, contact its reservations desk ahead of time to make preliminary reservations. Most establishments will hold reservations for a specified period of time so that you may notify your guests. The guests (unless told otherwise) should expect to pay for their accommodations.

Transportation

If out-of-town guests are flying to your wedding, offer to have a friend or family member pick them up at the airport. This is especially nice for someone who is not familiar with the area.

Different parts of the world have different transportation needs. If your wedding is being held atop a mountain bridge, making certain all of the guests get on the right train is an essential responsibility. See page 273 for information about transportation cards. Research which transportation methods are most time-effective and cost-effective for your out-of-town guests.

Rehearsal Dinner

It is also customary and polite to include out-of-town guests in the rehearsal dinner. The groom and his parents should send the invitations, ideally with directions or a map to the reception site. Dissuade out-of-town guests from attending the rehearsal.

Welcome Gift

Albeit optional, it is always a nice gesture to leave a welcoming gift in the rooms of out-of-town guests. The gifts can be identical for each guest (such as a basket of fruit, cheese, and crackers) or catered to the individual tastes of the guests (such as a bag of chips, nuts, and a six-pack of beer for the groom's college buddies).

Physically or Mentally Challenged Guests

If one or some of your guests are physically or mentally challenged, you will want to make it as easy as possible for them to attend your wedding. For example, send a friend or relative to pick up a mentally challenged guest and escort him/her directly to the wedding site.

Make certain to notify the ushers, if you are expecting a guest in a wheelchair, so that they can help this guest find a place to sit where they can see the proceedings and remain safe. If you are unsure where to have a guest in a wheelchair be seated, someone in charge of the facility will be able to direct you. Also, make certain the restrooms are equipped for persons with handicaps and be certain there is a permanent or rented ramp set up for guests in wheelchairs wherever stairs are present.

No Children, Please

Children can be so charming, but sometimes more formal weddings are not conducive to entertaining youngsters. In general, a toddler will not want to sit in a pew for two hours and behave as an adult. Elegant country clubs and hotels sometimes restrict children from dining in their ballrooms. Furthermore, the cost of a reception snowballs quickly when the guests include their children. You should also keep in mind that several guests might choose not to come to your reception if their children are not invited.

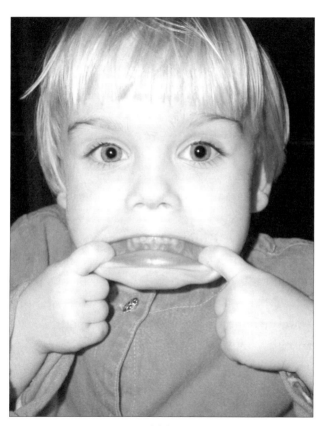

If you decide not to invite children to your wedding, this should be accomplished with as much grace as possible. First of all, do not include children's names on the invitation envelopes. Having "No children, please," or "Adults only," written or printed directly on the invitations is considered tacky. Do not make any exceptions to your rule beyond your own children, siblings, and the flower girl and ring bearer (if applicable).

Children Welcome

Or, if you decide it is acceptable for children to attend if they are supervised, it is acceptable to hire a local babysitter's services for the parents or assign someone ahead of time to be responsible for specific children, especially those who do not live nearby. The babysitter can watch the children off-site during the ceremony, in an adjoining room, in a nursery if held in a church, or in a corner of the same room in which the reception takes place.

Sometimes, the bride and groom have children, there are children in their family or circles-of-friends, or they simply adore children. If you want children to be an integral part of your wedding, cheers to you! Providing playthings and a play area is fitting for the reception, and letting them dance on the dance floor alongside adults will provide quality entertainment and memory making.

Once upon a time, a bride loved children so that her entire wedding embraced youth—both young in years and in heart. Her theme was playful and make-believe, held in an old castle's courtyard. Balls of all sizes, colors, and types covered the lawn, and the children delighted in playing together while the adults watched the ceremony.

If you decide to have children come to your wedding, these miniature adults might need some special attention, special foods, and special activities.

Responsible parents will keep a watchful eye on their offspring throughout the ceremony and reception. If the parents lose control of their children, you will be relieved to know that someone else (especially someone who does not know these parents and children) will undoubtedly say something to them. Of course, in the case of the crying baby at the wedding ceremony, the baby should immediately be removed until comforted.

As the bride and groom, even if the children get out of hand, try to portray a good-natured "kids will be kids" attitude and do not let the commotion spoil your wedding.

Those Closest

It is a nice gesture to send official invitations to the parents and the attendants, as they will want to keep theirs for a memento. You will want to keep an invitation for yourself as well, to put in a frame or in your wedding book.

Other Wedding Participants

You should send an invitation to the officiant and his or her spouse, but you need not send invitations to the florist, caterer, musicians, etc., unless they are your friends or relatives. Also, if another professional in your life, such as a therapist or doctor, has made a difference, a wedding invitation is a nice way to show your gratitude. Do not be disappointed, however, if he or she must decline to preserve the essence of the relationship.

Workplace

In the instance of an informal wedding, it is acceptable to post an invitation at work, perhaps on a bulletin board. Keep in mind that by doing so, everybody at your workplace, including their significant others and all of their children, might show up! For more formal events separate invitations must be sent to each coworker and their spouse or guest.

Wedding Guests and Reception Guests

Sometimes, the place you choose to get married is too small for everyone you hold dear. This is especially true in a very small church, in a chapel, on a boat, etc. Or, perhaps you choose to be wed someplace where strict guidelines exclude some of your guests from participating, such as in a religious temple. In this case, some brides and grooms re-enact the ring ceremony at the reception so those not included initially feel like they were more involved. If a portion of the guests will not be invited to the actual wedding ceremony, send to those people a reception invitation in place of a wedding invitation.

If you have a large guest list but cannot accommodate all of those guests at the wedding due to financial or area limitations, it is possible to invite most of the guests just to the reception. Simply send an invitation to those invited to the reception and enclose a separate card to those invited to the actual wedding. See page 242 for proper wording.

If you are having a home wedding, typically a reception occurs immediately after the wedding. It is only polite to invite everyone to both the wedding ceremony and the reception for a home wedding.

E-mail Invitations

It is considered bad form to send a wedding invitation via e-mail under any circumstances.

How Many to Expect

If you invite more than two hundred people to your wedding, you can expect 75% to 78% of them to actually attend. If you invite less than two hundred people, you can estimate that 80% to 85% will attend. However, factors such as how many people must travel, the date, and time of day must be taken into consideration. Of course, in the early stages of putting the wedding together, before any reply cards are returned, you should plan on everyone you have invited to attend.

Wording

The wording of the invitations should follow the formality and style of the wedding at hand. For highly formal weddings, some words take on more classic spellings, such as "favour" in lieu of "favor" and "honour" in lieu of "honor." Additionally, they are worded in the third person.

It is also important to remember that exact phrasing of the wedding announcement is highly dependent on local customs, social standing of the families, cultural background, and theme of the wedding. A tactful way to find out the best possible wording is to ask a trusted friend for some suggestions on where to have wedding announcements printed. By visiting the recommended print shops, it is possible to see examples of other well-received wedding announcements. Simply substitute your information in place of the words on the other invitation and you have a perfectly suitable invitation for your wedding.

While exact wording of the invitation may change slightly, the information needed to properly inform your guests about the wedding party, the time, and the location is standard.

Ceremony Only

Below find examples of how a formal invitation to the wedding ceremony only might be worded:

Mr. and Mrs. Justin Jones
request the honour of your presence
at the marriage of their daughter
Emily Nicole
to
Mr. Timothy Leonard Green
Friday, the eleventh of June,
at six o'clock in the evening
Washington Baptist Church
Atlanta, Georgia

Another way to word a formal invitation would be as follows:

Mr. and Mrs. Joshua Simpson
request the honour of your presence
at the marriage of their daughter
Hillary Elizabeth
to Mr. Andrew James Thornbird
on Thursday the sixteenth of June
at five o'clock
at The Church of the Good Shepherd
in the City of Dallas

Reception Only

If a certain number of the guests are invited to the reception, but not to the wedding ceremony, you may send those guests a reception invitation. A formal reception invitation can read:

Mr. and Mrs. Harvey Jepson
request the honour of your presence
at a reception celebrating
the marriage of their daughter
Kate Lynn

to

Mr. Randall Jay Osborne
Saturday, August twenty-first
at 7 o'clock in the evening
Georgetown City Park
Georgetown, California

Ceremony Plus Reception

If everyone on the guest list is invited to both the wedding ceremony and the reception, the below example of wording would work nicely:

> *Mr. and Mrs. Justin Jones*
> *request the honour of your presence*
> *at the marriage of their daughter*
> *Emily Nicole*
> *to*
> *Mr. Timothy Leonard Green*
> *Friday, the eleventh of June,*
> *at six o'clock in the evening*
> *Washington Baptist Church*
> *and afterward*
> *at the Cotton Heights Country Club*
> *Atlanta, Georgia*

If the wedding is highly formal, a separate card should be sent for the wedding and another sent announcing the reception. It is also customary for the announcements in highly formal weddings to be sent in double envelopes with vellum or tissue paper covering the invitation. In some circles, the invitations even have to be engraved or embossed rather than just printed. Some people go so far as to have their invitations foil stamped. Properly done, foil stamped invitations are magnificently beautiful and elegant. These customs are still observed in some form in most areas, but new styles in wedding invitations are slowly replacing the formal and very costly traditional announcements. *Note: If the wedding is more informal, "the pleasure of your company" works well in lieu of "the honour of your presence."*

A more contemporary way to word a formal wedding invitation is as follows:

Please join us
on the joyous occasion
when our daughter
Samantha
will be married to
Bradley O'Dell
on Friday, the ninth of January
at seven o'clock
Main Street Gardens
Phoenix, Arizona

Military

If the bride and/or groom would like to use their military titles in their wedding invitation, they can do so. If the groom's rank is at least Lieutenant Commander in the Navy or Coast Guard and at least Major in any other armed forces, his title comes before his name.

Lieutenant Commander David Stevens
United States Navy

Noncommissioned service people can use their titles, too, if they please. (The exact title is optional.)

Sally Marie
Corporal, United States Army

Divorced Parents

If the bride's parents are divorced, both their names can appear on the invitation as the hosts (if they agree to it), or the parent's name who is primarily hosting the wedding can appear singly. For the former, the mother's name appears first, and on its own line. If unmarried, the bride's mother's maiden name may precede her married name, indicating that she is divorced (Mrs. O'Neill Stetson). If remarried, she uses her new married name (Mrs. Jorge Gonzales). If widowed, she would use her married name (Mrs. Rick Stetson). Of course, so many circumstances exist that there is no steadfast rule about how the names appear on the invitation. What is mentioned here is merely the most traditional, serving as a foundation to help you make your own best choice.

Cohosts

In Spain, it is customary for the fathers of the bride and groom to issue their children's wedding invitations jointly because both families contribute substantially to the cost of the wedding. Having both the bride's and the groom's parents pay for their children's wedding is beginning to gain popularity in other parts of the world. If this is the case for your wedding, the bride or her mother should ask the groom's parents if they would like their names to appear on the invitations. Some people will be thrilled about the idea, while others who are more traditional might ask that the invitations not be issued jointly. With the groom's parents' permission, both sets of parents' names should appear on the invitation, with the bride's parents coming first.

A way to word this follows:

> *Mr. and Mrs. Gregory Heineken*
> *and*
> *Mr. and Mrs. Edward Stevenson*
> *request the pleasure of your company*
> *at the marriage of their children*
> *Natasha Eileen*
> *and*
> *Mr. Eugene Mahlon Stevenson*
> *Marriage to be celebrated*
> *at*
> *St. John's Cathedral*
> *1647 Church Street*

Someone Other Than Parents Hosting

If other relatives or friends besides the bride's parents are hosting the wedding, their names and relationship to the bride are mentioned on the invitation. If anyone other than a relative is giving the wedding, no relationship is mentioned. Sporadically, the groom's parents hold the wedding, and if so, the first part of the invitation can be worded:

Mr. and Mrs. Zachary Black
request the pleasure of your company
at the marriage of
Abigail Valerie McCune
to
Mr. Zachary Ayden Black, Jr.

Bride and Groom Hosting

If the bride and groom are financing and responsible for their own wedding (which is becoming more commonplace), here is a nice way to word the more formal invitation:

> *Georgia Povich*
> *and*
> *Marshall Erickson*
> *request the honour of your presence*
> *at their*
> *Marriage Ceremony*
> *Friday, the tenth of December*
> *at eleven o'clock*
> *Saint Joseph's Church*
> *Lakeview, Washington*

A more contemporary way to word an invitation for a wedding given by the bride and groom:

Kelly Thompson

and

Jeremy Hamilton

invite you to share their joy

when on Saturday, the twenty-sixth of July

at four o'clock

they exchange marriage vows

in a celebration of love

R.S.V.P.

R.S.V.P. means *repondez s'il vous plait* in French, and is translated in English to mean respond if you please. Generally, an R.S.V.P. is not necessary for the wedding ceremony itself, but it is an effective way to determine how many guests to expect at the reception. Therefore, some reception cards (or combined wedding and reception invitations) have R.S.V.P. printed on the bottom, indicating that a response is desired.

R.S.V.P. can be spelled in all capitals, or with just the R capitalized. Periods appear after each of the four letters. Or, you can simply have Please respond printed on the bottom of the invitation, if you prefer.

Punctuation

Periods appear only after title and name abbreviations such as "Mr." and "Jr." Additionally, a period can be used in an abbreviation used for an official name of a city (Ft. Collins), church (St. Mary's), and so forth.

Use a comma after the day of the week (Saturday, the twenty-second of December).

Abbreviations

There should be no abbreviations on a wedding invitation except for titles before names (Mr. and Mrs.). "Junior" may be abbreviated, for the same reason (Jr.). "Miss" and "Master" are written in full. "Doctor" is typically written out in full for a medical doctor, unless the name following is so lengthy that it does not fit in the allotted space or on a single line. An academic "doctor" who always uses Ph.D. following his or her name would not use Doctor. Most would leave Ph.D. off. "The Reverend" and military titles are written in full.

If a host or the bride or groom goes by a nickname and few people would recognize his or her formal first name, it is acceptable to put the nickname in parenthesis after the formal first name. So, if Theodore goes by Tito, his name would read: Mr. Theodore (Tito) Anderson.

The Time

In the evening, or in the afternoon, or in the morning are all used in place of a.m. or p.m. However, six o'clock would mean the wedding starts at 6:00 p.m., so (indicating the time of day is unnecessary. It is a safe bet that a wedding would not begin at 6:00 in the morning!

The Year

On any wedding invitation, having the year printed is up to you. Many people omit the year, but if your wedding is scheduled for a month at the end or beginning of the year, it might be a good idea to include it. The year is always spelled out, as in two thousand and four.

Nontraditional

The aforementioned instructions have been written about the wording found in traditional wedding invitations. Nontraditional invitations can be created that are as charming as traditional invitations, with the added benefit of warmth that can only come from the heart. With a nontraditional invitation, the wording can take on any shape and go in any direction—whether similar to a traditional invitation or not—just so long as it is tasteful. Poems, song lyrics, thoughts directly from the minds of the bride and groom, etc., are all found written in nontraditional invitations. Also, some invitations incorporate a photograph of the bride and groom.

Appearance

Traditional folded wedding invitations measure approximately 5½ by 7½ inches, and nonfolded invitations measure about 4½ by 5½ inches. Formal invitations can be engraved, thermographed (which costs considerably less, yet appears similar to engraving), or printed in black ink. The paper is high quality and usually white or cream-colored.

Pretty, elegant fonts—either script or block—are acceptable, as long as they are not too fancy to be legible. The writing is centered on the paper, and there is no period after the last word (even though it reads like a sentence). Commas are used to enhance readability, and line breaks separate different bits of information. For example, the day of week and date usually appear on a line above the time. Also, the bride's name appears on its own line, as does the groom's name. See page 251 for an example.

A nontraditional wedding invitation might be printed in any color of ink on any color or type of paper, as long as it looks nice and is readable. Also, nontraditional invitations take on many different shapes (a heart, for instance) and might include some type of artwork or photograph. Also, while more traditional invitations are written line-by-line, each line being centered on the page, nontraditional and more informal invitations can be in paragraph form. A couple of examples indicating how an informal invitation might be phrased are as follows: the first being written by the bride herself, the second written by the bride's mother.

Dear Aunt Brenda,

Roberto and I are getting married in the Snowbird Chapel in Austin on Thursday, April seventeenth, at ten o'clock. We hope you can join us for the wedding and brunch afterward at Mom's house.

Yours very sincerely,
Isabella

My Dear Mr. and Mrs. Johnson,

Betty and Jeffrey are to be married at home on Tuesday, December eleventh, at eleven o'clock. We hope very much that you will be able to attend the wedding and stay for a light lunch with our families and closest friends.

Affectionately,
Julie Morton

Mention of Gifts

These days, couples oftentimes register at local and national stores and shops for gifts they would like to receive for their wedding or showers. See page 143 for more about registering for gifts. While invitations you receive to weddings sometimes indicate where the couple is registered (usually in smaller print at the very bottom), this practice is inappropriate. It is also in poor taste for the invitation to hint that the couple would rather receive money in lieu of a wedding gift. Simply put, it is considered impolite to mention gifts at all on a wedding invitation.

The exceptions are if gifts are not desired at all (common especially for second marriages or marriages between people who are older and well-established), or if the couple wants wedding guests to make donations to their chosen charity.

Envelopes

The best etiquette for addressing wedding invitation envelopes is to do so neatly by hand, in black ink. Traditionally, the bride and her bridesmaids or other close girlfriends address the envelopes. Sometimes, the bride will hire a professional calligrapher or appoint a friend or relative with especially pretty handwriting to do the job.

Address Labels

With the onset of computers and word processors, wedding invitations with address labels stuck on their envelopes show up in mailboxes quite frequently. Using address labels is slowly gaining acceptance and favor, especially because there are a large variety of fonts available that make the envelopes appear to be handwritten. The names and addresses of the guests can be entered into a spreadsheet on a personal computer and regenerated and adjusted for pre-wedding event invitations and thank-you cards later on.

If you decide to take this modern route with addressing envelopes, use clear labels (unless you can find a label the exact color of your envelope) and a pretty and legible font, one similar to the font used for the invitations, or purchase fancy labels that match the wedding style at paper or scrapbook stores.

Still, using address labels might offend your guests who see it as impersonal. Many etiquette experts still recommend that envelopes are addressed by hand.

Return Address

Putting a return address on the envelope is necessary, and while handwriting the return address is most favorable, some opt to have the return address printed on the left-hand corner or back flap of the envelope. Most printers offer this option when wedding invitations are ordered. Preprinted return addresses save time, and like address labels, are gaining acceptance.

Addressing Tips

- For each person who is invited to the wedding, his or her name should appear on the envelope.
- For families with young children, the children's names (or "and family") should appear on the invitation behind their parents' names, if they are indeed invited.
- If children are not invited, omit their names entirely.
- If children live in the household but are over sixteen years old, they should receive an invitation separate from their parents.
- For married, engaged, and dating couples that live together, it is in good taste to include the significant other's name on the invitation.
- If dating couples live at separate addresses, it is best to send a separate invitation to each individual.

- If a prospective guest is unattached at the time you send invitations, it is okay to write "and guest" on the invitation, which tells the person he or she has permission to bring a date or friend along.

Inner and Outer

Sometimes two envelopes are used for wedding invitations, especially those that are more formal in nature. If you choose to have two envelopes for your invitations, the outer envelope is stamped and addressed to the main recipient(s), and the inner envelope (which is not sealed) shows the names of the main recipient(s) plus the names or mention of children or dates. As mentioned earlier, with highly formal invitations, vellum or tissue paper is placed over the card.

The outer envelope would read:

Mr. and Mrs. Christopher Clarke and family
1523 Old Oak Lane
Orlando, Florida 33298

The inner envelope reads:

Mr. and Mrs. Clarke
Allison, James and Courtney

Or, the outer envelope might read:

Mr. James Holding
9942 Waterway Street
New York, New York 10002

And the inner envelope reads:

Mr. Holding and guest

Abbreviations

For formal and semiformal invitations, full, formal names should be written on the envelopes, whenever possible. For example, the use of initials or nicknames is generally frowned upon. If you are uncertain what someone's full name is (perhaps he goes by "Spanky" but you suspect that might be a nickname), a quick phone call to someone who would know, or the person himself, will alleviate any question. As with the invitation itself, "Mr." and "Mrs." and "Ms." are always abbreviated, but "Miss," "Master," "The Reverend," and "Doctor" are written out in full. "Junior" can be written in full or abbreviated to "Jr." States and military titles are also spelled out on a formal invitation's envelope, even if the military person is retired.

Reception Card

If the wedding and reception are being held in different locations, or if the reception is scheduled several hours after the wedding ceremony, it is recommended that a reception card be enclosed with the invitation. For everyone invited to the reception, simply slip a small reception card in the invitation. Information such as the location and time of the reception is outlined on this card.

Below a sample of how a reception card might read:

Reception
Immediately following the ceremony
Endeavors Hotel and Casino
Las Vegas, Nevada
R.s.v.p.

Wedding Ceremony Card

This same format can be used for a card to invite selected guests to attend the wedding ceremony.

Map Enclosure

If the wedding ceremony or reception takes place somewhere that the guests might have a difficult time finding, a map enclosure is helpful. The map can be included in invitations going to out-of-town guests only, if you feel local guests know where the sites are located.

Map enclosures are a single piece of paper, and a neatly drawn or computer-generated map is printed on one side. If desired, the word-by-word directions can be printed on the opposite side or you may include a helpful picture of the reception site so guests know what facility to look for.

Pew Card

You can send pew cards to those special friends and relatives whom you wish to sit in the first few rows at the wedding. These cards can indicate the row a seat is reserved in their honor, as seen below:

Please present this card to an usher
Pew Number Four
on Friday the sixth of November

or

Pew 6
Mr. Alexander Henry Jones

Sometimes, special guests are seated "within the ribbons," which means the bride and groom wish for them to sit in the rows at the front of the church, which are sectioned off with a ribbon (usually white). A seating card that would appear in the invitations for these special guests reads something like this:

> *Within the Ribbons*
> *Friday the sixth of November*

At Home Card

If the bride and groom are moving to a new residence, or will be away honeymooning for an extended period of time after their wedding, it is proper and convenient to include an "At Home" card in the wedding invitation.

This card reads along the lines of:

> *Mr. and Mrs. Walker*
> *will be at home*
> *after July 4*
> *1234 Oak Lane*
> *New York, NY 10003*

"At Home" cards are small enough to fit inside the wedding invitation, like the reception card.

Reply Card

If knowing how many guests plan on attending is important information for you to know by a certain date, enclosing a reply card might ensure a more accurate and timely count than relying on everybody to RSVP on their own device. Giving the guests a timeline can be effective (prodding those folks who are notorious procrastinators) or offensive to some traditionalists who feel all your other guests should be as dependable as they, themselves, are. Anyway, below find an example of how a reply card may be worded when the responses need to be accurate and timely:

> *Please respond by the twelfth of February*
> *M* _____
> *will__ attend*

If a reply card is used, it should be included within the wedding and/or reception invitation, along with a stamped and addressed envelope. The envelope, much smaller than the invitation envelope(s), should be addressed to whomever is sponsoring the wedding. Usually, the printed wedding stationery items will match one another.

Below is another example of a reply card:

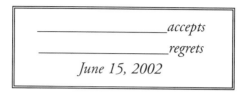

_____*accepts*

_____*regrets*

June 15, 2002

A third option for a reply card is a blank note with something as simple as "The favour of a reply is requested," printed at the bottom. This allows space for the guests to write a quick note along with the information that they can or cannot make it. Again, a stamped/addressed envelope accompanies the reply card.

Transportation Card

If the wedding takes place somewhere way out-of-the-way, or in terrain difficult for an ordinary vehicle to access, or in a facility where parking is limited, special transportation will need to be arranged so the guests can be easily transported to the wedding site. If special transportation is mandated, there will be a card in the invitation describing the procedure, including any information necessary for the guest to gain access to the area from which the transportation is leaving. A sample of such a card is located just below:

A train will leave the Clinton Train Station at 2:00 P.M.
and arrive in Bountiful at 2:25 P.M.
Returning train will leave Bountiful at 5:00 P.M.
and arrive at the Clinton Train Station at 5:25 P.M.
This card is your pass.

Stamps

There is always a first-class stamp on the outer envelope, and if you insert a reply card, its envelope is also stamped. There are a multitude of different designs of stamps available, and if you can get one that has a romantic theme or feel, this is best. If you notice a style of stamp that is especially appealing to you, you might want to buy it right away, in case it becomes difficult to find. If the wedding revolves around a holiday theme, such as St. Valentine's Day or Christmas, you might want to use holiday stamps. For ease, you will want to choose self-adhesive stamps in lieu of the ones you have to lick.

While you are at the post office choosing stamps, have an invitation, complete with all inserts, weighed to see if it requires more than one stamp. If your wedding invitation package weighs more or is larger than what a single stamp covers, adhere two stamps on each outer envelope. Do not have your envelopes metered; this looks less than personal and elegant.

If you are having a large wedding, you will want to ask the post office how they would like you to organize the invitations to make the process run smoothest for them. Some post offices will gladly let you use one of their plastic mail crates to carry your invitations to them. Be aware that new postal requirements for bar-code stickers will be a consideration on the outer mailing envelopes.

Frequent postal rate increases have affected current invitation etiquette. You will want to inquire as to whether or not the stamp rate will increase by the time the reply cards are mailed back, if applicable. You do not want your potential guests to have to supplement the stamp on their own accord. Plus, some potential guests might mail the reply card with insufficient postage, causing a delay in reaching its destination. Such delays can alter guest counts, causing frantic last minute adjustments.

Packaging the Invitations

Reply cards, if being used, should be stuffed into their own little envelope, which is addressed to the hosts of the wedding, stamped, and left unsealed.

If the wedding invitation is a folded style, insert all of the enclosures (reception cards, reply cards, pew cards, at-home cards, maps and directions) within the invitation. It is best if the enclosures match the invitation.

Folded invitations go fold first into the inner envelope (or outer envelope, if an inner envelope is not being used). If the invitation is not folded, slip it into the envelope with the print toward the flap. That way, the printed side shows when the envelope is opened. An inner envelope is left unsealed, and the outer envelope is always sealed and stamped. When inserting an inner envelope into an outer envelope, both flaps should be at the top.

Pieces of Mail Not Enclosed in the Wedding Invitations

Save the Date Cards

If you are planning your wedding months in advance during a particularly busy time of year, sending "Save the Date" cards is a nice tool for informing your future guests about the wedding. Hopefully, they will mark the date on their calendar so they do not make conflicting plans. These cards should match the wedding invitations in style and tone, and they should not be sent during busy holiday weeks.

A Save the Date card can be worded:

> *Save the Date*
> *Joy Beckworth*
> *and*
> *Gordon Wilson*
> *have chosen*
> *June 7, 2002*
> *as the day of their wedding*

There are other, more novel ideas to get the date on potential guests' calendars. For example, for an informal wedding the information can be printed on a cute magnet, serving as a reminder on people's refrigerators. (Check with the local post office to see if current postal regulations permit the mailing of magnets.) Or, "Joy and Gordon's Wedding" can be printed on a sticker, ready to be stuck on the wedding date on people's calendars.

Accommodation Information Cards

It is customary for the bride and her parents or the groom and his parents to provide accommodation information for their out-of-town family and friends, such as prices, and deadlines for reservations, transportation possibilities, ect. Sometimes, out-of-town family and friends stay in the homes of the bride or groom's parents. Or, local family members and friends might offer their homes to out-of-town guests. If not, the bride and groom should make hotel or motel reservations on their behalf, and send all pertinent and helpful information on a card in plenty of time for arrangements to be made.

Wedding Announcements

Announcements are sent to anyone the bride or groom knows fairly well who is not invited to the wedding or reception. They are also sent to the bride's and groom's family and friends, in the case of an elopement. Announcements are especially helpful for professional people who wish to notify clients or business associates of their change in marital status and/or name.

The announcements should be engraved, if at all possible. The extra time and expense of engraving should be thoroughly considered. Announcements should be mailed shortly after the wedding, but it is acceptable to send announcements up to a year afterward. Even though the woman might have taken her husband's last name, the announcements should still bear her maiden name.

It is not necessary for someone to give the couple a wedding gift when he or she receives an announcement; but if a gift is sent, do send a thank-you note as soon as possible.

Below is an example of how an announcement might read:

> *Mr. and Mrs. Mark Caldwell*
> *have the pleasure of announcing*
> *the marriage of their daughter*
> *Natalie*
> *to*
> *Ryan Bartles*
> *Saturday, the thirtieth of November,*
> *Two thousand two*
> *Denver, Colorado*

If the couple sends the announcement themselves, it should read something like:

Paulette O'Malley
and
Jordan Clark
have the pleasure to
announce their marriage
Sunday, the second of March,
Two thousand two
Atlanta, Georgia

Chapter Seven: Service Providers

Photography

Because your wedding photographs will capture the experience of your wedding—perhaps even better than your memories of it—it is imperative that you hire or appoint a competent photographer. If you do not know a good wedding photographer in your area, ask your family and friends for recommendations, and search the internet or phone book.

The Photographer

Once you find a potentially good photographer, schedule a meeting with him or her to look at their portfolios of other people's weddings. Asking for references is always a very good idea. If possible, meet with more than one photographer so you can compare the quality of their work and the prices they charge. Keep in mind that just because someone is a first-rate portrait photographer does not necessarily mean that he or she is a first-rate wedding photographer.

You will need to decide if you want the same photographer that covers your wedding and reception to take the formal bridal photographs several months before the wedding date. You might want to have a portrait photographer with a different artistic style take the bridal photographs.

You need a photographer who has no qualms about taking candid photographs of people he or she probably does not know. You need someone who is good with children, if children are involved in your wedding. You need someone equipped to handle the lighting issues of your wedding and reception locations, whether they be indoors or outside, and you will probably want one who has the equipment to take both black-and-white as well as color photographs. Most importantly, you need a photographer who will listen to what you want; after all, it is a record of your wedding day.

Wedding Packages

Ask to see a list of the photographer's wedding packages, if he or she has them instated. If you see one you are interested in, you will want to inquire as to how much he or she charges for add-on's, or if the proofs can be purchased. How many photographs does the photographer estimate taking? Are black-and-whites included with the colors? Is sepia-tone photography desirable? What will the finish on the photos look like? How long does the photographer typically stay at a reception? How long before proofs can be viewed? When will final photographs be available?

Another important item to discuss is who will actually be taking the photographs. Sometimes, popular professional photographers send their assistant, or an up-and-coming photographer who is building a portfolio, to the weddings; and that particular person did not take the photographs in the portfolios you perused.

Familiar Photographer

If you are lucky enough to have a good friend or family member who is a professional or talented photographer, he or she might offer to take your wedding photographs, perhaps as a wedding gift. This is quite a nice offer, especially since professional wedding photographs typically cost in the neighborhood of $1,000 and more. If you decide to accept their offer, you can offer to pay for the film and developing.

If your friend or you are the slightest bit nervous about such an arrangement, suggest hiring a professional photographer in addition. In most cases, the more photographs the better!

Picturing the Special Guests

Once you find and book a photographer you are happy with, you should designate a friend or family member to approach the photographer at the wedding and point out people who are especially important to you. Hopefully, with direction, the photographer will try to take at least one photograph of a majority of your guests. Otherwise, he or she might concentrate on a group of people the bride and groom hardly know, just because they are photogenic, beautifully dressed, or simply beautiful people. If children are invited to the wedding, the photographer might be asked to get some candid shots of them.

Picture Perfect

Below are additional pointers for making certain your photographs adequately represent your wedding day:

- Have the photographer take candid photographs before the actual ceremony. This includes the dressing room (once everybody is decently dressed), the groom and groomsmen as they wait in anticipation, and so forth.

- Have formal photographs taken, including at a very minimum: bride and groom; bride, groom, and bridesmaids including flower girl; bride, groom, and entire wedding party; bride, groom, and bride's parents; bride, groom, and groom's parents.

- If you wish, have formal photographs taken of: bride, groom, and groomsmen/ushers including ring bearer.

- Make certain the photographer is stationed in an inconspicuous place while the ceremony is being performed, like the back of the church or off to the side.

- Ask him or her to take photographs of the wedding party during both the wedding procession and the return down the aisle following the ceremony.

- Do not have the photographer get too close to the altar (or wherever the vows are being exchanged), as this can be quite bothersome and distracting.

- Do not allow guests to take flash photographs while the ceremony is taking place. This is rarely a problem, but if it comes up, have an usher politely ask the guest to refrain from flash photography, as it is distracting and can potentially impair the professional photography.

- If you wish, place throwaway cameras on the tables at the reception. The guests will enjoy snapping photos of each other and the reception events. Designate a friend to collect the cameras at the end of the evening.

Videography

An additional way to commemorate your wedding day is by having it videotaped. You will have fun watching it after your honeymoon and on a wedding anniversary. Also, it is nice to show your wedding video to a special person in your life who, for whatever reason, was unable to attend in person. For example, copies of the video can be mailed to friends or relatives living in distant locations, allowing them to share in your special day. Furthermore, your younger or future children will delight in seeing the wedding on videotape. A styled-to-music version is ideal.

Research

Sometimes, the photo studio you hire to take your wedding photographs works in partnership with a specific video cameraperson. If not, the research involved in finding a good video cameraperson is similar to finding a good photographer.

Video Cameraperson

You will want to ask the video cameraperson to show you ample videos of other weddings he or she has produced. Pay keen attention to the flow of the video, and whether or not the overall video style suits your wedding style. The editing should be clean, the picture and sound clear. It is a good idea to ask for references.

Wedding Packages

Some video tapers offer wedding packages, which might include videotaping the bride and her attendants getting dressed, interviews of the guests, the ceremony, and the reception—along with a variety of price ranges based upon number of final videos you want, special effects, background music, and so forth.

Rules

If you are getting married in a church, you will want to ask the clergyperson about whether or not the entire ceremony may be videotaped. Also, you might have the video cameraperson come to the wedding setting before the wedding date. He or she can find a good place to videotape, where a majority of the ceremony can be captured on tape without being too obtrusive to the ceremony.

Familiar Video Cameraperson

If a good friend offers to videotape your wedding as a gift, that is great. Like a friend who offers to take the wedding photographs, offer to pay for the videotaping expenses. If you do not feel confident that your friend will do a superior job, or if your friend is a bit uncertain him- or herself, see what your friend thinks about your hiring a professional to videotape in addition. If the videotaping is done as a gift, you can make a few suggestions, such as which parts of the wedding you would like covered—but do not go overboard on suggestions or orders.

While having a professional video of your wedding is a nice addition, if your budget is strained (expect to pay a professional anywhere from $200–$1,500), opt for asking a special friend to tape the wedding home-movie style. It is best to select someone familiar with the process of using a video camcorder. While the final product might not be as professional as if you hired an experienced and highly equipped video cameraperson, it will still be a reminder of your wedding. Plus, you can always have it professionally edited at a later date.

Flowers

Flowers are an intrinsic part of almost every wedding, regardless of faith or culture. Whether the bride carries a single white rose or calla lily down the aisle, or a fancy, colorful bouquet with flowers and ribbons cascading to her knees, flowers play a vital role in supporting the style and formality of the occasion. After the style, color scheme, and location of the wedding and reception have been determined, it is time to think of flowers. Often the symbolic nature of flowers matters in some cultures.

Flowers of the Season

Following is a list of popular wedding flowers, many of which can be found year-round. Of course, you will need to talk to a local florist to determine which ones are available for the wedding date you have chosen. Out-of-season flowers are much more costly and do not stay fresh for as long.

Flowers	Season
Acacia	Winter
Asters	Fall
Baby's Breath	All
Bachelor Buttons	All
Bells of Ireland	Summer
Camellias	Winter
Carnations	All
Cornflowers	All
Chrysanthemums	Fall
Dahlias	Fall
Daisies	Summer
Delphiniums	All
Forget-me-nots	Spring
Gardenias	All
Gladioli	All
Ivy	All
Jonquils	Spring
Lilacs	Winter or Spring
Lilies	All

Flowers	Season
Orchids	All
Peonies	Summer
Poinsettias	Winter
Sweetheart Roses	All
Queen Anne's Lace	Summer
Roses	All
Snapdragons	All
Stephanotis	All
Sweet Peas	Summer or Spring
Tulips	Spring
Violets	Spring
Zinnias	Fall

Symbolic Meanings of Certain Flowers

Acacia	Friendship
Anemone	Anticipation
Apple Blossom	Good Fortune
Bluebell	Truth

Carnation	Distinction
Crocus	Joy
Daisy	Innocence
Forget-me-not	True Love
Gardenia	Happiness
Holly	Happiness at Home
Honeysuckle	Faithfulness
Lily of the Valley	Purity
Orange Blossom	Purity and Fertility
Orchid	Beauty
Pansy	Good Thoughts
Rose	Love
Rosemary	Commitment
Sage	Virtue
Sweet Pea	Pleasure, Daintiness
Violet	Modesty
Xeranthemum	Cheerfulness & Optimism
Water Lily	Pure in Heart
Zinnia	Friendship

Flowers by the Month

January	Carnation
February	Violet
March	Jonquil
April	Sweet Pea
May	Lily of the Valley
June	Rose
July	Larkspur
August	Gladiolus
October	Aster
November	Chrysanthemum
December	Narcissus

Fresh vs Artificial (Silk, Paper, Dried)

Below is a list weighing the benefits and disadvantages of using fresh and artificial flowers.

Fresh Flowers

Positive

Naturally beautiful; wonderfully fragrant; everyone loves fresh flowers.

Negative

Hot weather wilts flowers; limited to selection of flowers on hand and in season; they eventually die, sometimes right after the wedding; must be arranged and delivered shortly before the wedding.

Artificial Flowers

Positive

Can be put together with a wider variety of arrangements since water is unnecessary; can use any type of flowers, whether in season or not; will last forever; can be arranged well in advance of wedding.

Negative

Can look fake; not fragrant; some people think using artificial flowers is in poor taste.

Either or . . .

Whether using fresh or artificial flowers for your wedding, you will discover that both can be costly. Make certain that your wedding budget allots adequate room for floral expenditures. To help control costs, use care when selecting fresh flowers. Some types of flowers (notably the rare and out-of-season) are very expensive, while others—some of which are equally beautiful—are reasonably priced. As for artificial flowers, you will want to use those that appear as lifelike as possible. Realistic-looking flowers made of silk can be expensive, yet inexpensive fabric or plastic flowers create the wrong atmosphere for a beautiful wedding.

Both

Some weddings are decorated with a mixture of fresh and artificial flowers. For instance, while the bouquets and decorative accent flowers are artificial (so they will retain their beauty), the corsages, and boutonnieres are fresh. Or, if a bride desires a certain flower that is too costly or simply unattainable, she might supplement a fresh bouquet with a few lifelike artificial blossoms. Be mindful not to choose a type of flower that looks too out-of-place or out-of-season for your wedding. A red rose looks perfectly lovely throughout the year, but a yellow tulip looks peculiar in a December wedding. Also, more formal flowers such as orchids and calla lilies are appropriate for formal weddings, but not so much for casual weddings.

Creative Substitutes

If your wedding style is more whimsical, you can use flowers made of paper, colorful beads, or anything that strikes your creative mind. Some florists use real and artificial fruits, pretty ribbons, and costume jewels in their floral creations. Twigs, herbs, brightly colored leaves, and berries make delightful floral arrangements and bouquets for autumn weddings. Imagine the surprise of glittery snowflake bouquets for a winter wonderland wedding.

Coordinating

Whether fresh or artificial, flowers should complement the color(s), texture, shape, and style of the bride and bridesmaid's dresses. For instance, if the bride's dress is long, sleek, and elegant, a tiny nosegay bouquet appears small and insignificant. Likewise, if the bridesmaids wear fluffy, knee-length, lilac dresses, a large, cascading bouquet of red blossoms looks unattractive. If beautiful beading wraps around the waist of the bride's dress, a crescent-shaped bouquet would work nicely, while a large nosegay would hide the beadwork. Bridesmaid dresses made of flowery material look best with simple, monochromatic bouquets.

If you are unsure what type of bouquet will look nice with the wedding dresses, florists usually have suitable suggestions. Photographs or material swatches of the dresses aid the florist in making such recommendations. The florist will also want to take into account the height of the bride and the bridesmaids. A petite bride does not want to have to worry about stepping on her large, cascading bouquet, and a little whisper of a bouquet might be invisible against a tall bride's long gown. However, a single long-stemmed flower is lovely.

More or Less

Before visiting a florist, you will need to have an idea as to how many flowers you need. For example, if you want to have your June wedding in the city park, where hundreds of beautiful flowers bloom each summer, your need for flowers will be quite minimal—a bouquet for the bride and each of her attendants; corsages for the mothers, grandmothers, and other special female guests; boutonnieres for the groom, his groomsmen, fathers, and grandfathers. On the other hand, if you are getting married in a church with gorgeous stained-glass windows and stately wooden pews, you will want to order more flowers to include pew marker flowers, an arrangement for the altar, arrangements for the foyer and guest book table, and so forth. Likewise, if the reception takes place outdoors or someplace already elaborately decorated, the need for flowers diminishes as

opposed to the floral needs of a bare party room in the back of a restaurant. If the florist previews the wedding site, he or she can visualize what type and how many flowers will look the best.

Start with the basic flower needs, and then if your budget allows, add more flowers as you wish. Usually, the bride and her family pay for all of the flowers. Sometimes, she is responsible for most of the flowers, with the groom being responsible for paying for the corsages for their mothers as well as the boutonnieres for their fathers and his groomsmen. In some areas, it is traditional for the groom to pay for the bride's bouquet and her going-away corsage. Whether the bride pays the entire florist bill, or the groom pays a portion, it is recommended that all of the flowers be ordered with the same florist to ensure consistent quality and to simplify matters.

Bride's Bouquet

If the bride wishes to perform in the popular tradition of the bouquet toss (see page 424), she can toss her original bouquet, or she can have an alternate bouquet made solely for the purpose of tossing to the lucky unmarried lady. Also, if she wants to wear a corsage as she and her groom leave the reception, a corsage can be fitted into the bride's bouquet and removed when the reception winds down.

Preserving the Bride's Bouquet

There are several techniques for preserving the bridal bouquet, if the bride is interested in doing so. Drying, pressing, and potpourri are all good ways to enjoy the bouquet awhile longer. If you are not familiar with these processes, simply ask your florist or visit a local craft store. Some brides choose silk in the first place.

Bridal Party Flowers

The bride's attendants carry bouquets similar to her own, but usually smaller in size. The bridesmaid's bouquets can be identical to one another, if so desired. Sometimes, the maid/matron of honor holds a bouquet with a few more flowers than the other bridesmaids' bouquets. If a junior bridesmaid is appointed, she might carry a smaller bouquet (especially if she is rather young). A flower girl can carry a small bouquet similar to the bridesmaids', or she can hold a basket of flowers. If floral headpieces are desired for the bride and/or her attendants and flower girl, they should be ordered with the other flowers.

It is important to order arrangements for table settings that are in keeping with the other bridal flowers.

Corsages

It is customary for the bride and groom to provide their mothers, stepmothers, and grandmothers with lovely corsages immediately before the wedding. Their corsages should coordinate with the color of the dress they will wear. If they do not know what color they will be wearing, order a simple corsage in basic white or cream, something that goes with everything.

Not only can a corsage be pinned to the shoulder, it can be designed to be worn around the wrist, on the waistline, or pinned onto a purse or hat. It is a nice idea to ask if the women have a preference as to what type of corsage they prefer since a silk dress or another fine fabric is likely to be ruined by floral pins and the weight of a corsage.

In addition, any close female friends who attend the guest book, recite a poem, or sing a solo for the ceremony can be presented with a corsage or other floral accessory. In general, it is a nice gesture for the bride and groom to give any exceptionally important and special lady a corsage to wear for their wedding.

Boutonnieres

Long ago, a bride would take a single flower from her bouquet and pin it on her beloved groom. Today, a groom's boutonniere is usually made from a single flower chosen from the bridal bouquet. Fathers, grandfathers, ushers, groomsmen, and the ring bearer also wear boutonnieres, which should look different from the groom's. As with corsages, it is a nice gesture to order a boutonniere for a man who is a special relative or wedding helper. A boutonniere is pinned to the lapel of a jacket. Flowers commonly made into boutonnieres include carnations, lily of the valley, and roses.

The Cake

Also, as soon as you have ordered your wedding cake, the florist can create floral accents for the cake itself, as well as for the cake table. See pages 297–302.

Music

Like most of the people you hire to make your wedding truly wonderful, you will need to book musicians for your wedding ceremony and reception at the earliest time possible. The best musicians fill their calendars far in advance. This is particularly important if dancing is to be part of your reception plans.

Research

If you do not personally know any musicians that you feel will play appropriately for your wedding, ask friends and family members, the music department head at a nearby college, and church group leaders for referrals. The tone of your wedding will be an important issue for you and the musicians to agree on. You want them to dress in keeping with your plan. Look on the internet or in the phone book for information about musical groups living nearby. Or, attend local band concerts and other musical performances to see if their music suits your needs. Sometimes, radio station and nightclub deejays moonlight as wedding reception deejays. You can also contact a local music store or music teacher, or the local musicians union (which can be found in the phone book or on the internet).

Types of Music

Almost every wedding has some kind of music being played during the wedding ceremony. This can be the church pianist or organist, a friend who plays the cello or violin, a string quartet, a soloist, a keyboard player, an orchestra, a band, and even a collection of tapes or CDs being played over a home stereo system.

The music selections should match the style and formality of the wedding. For example, if the wedding is on an island paradise, you might choose to have local islanders drumming and strumming in the background. If your wedding will take place in a church, you will need to talk to the clergy-person to make certain your music selections follow regulations, if any are instated.

Ceremony Music

Music is typically played during the ceremony as the guests are taking their seats, as much as an hour before the actual ceremony is scheduled to commence. Also, music is played at the processional, as the wedding party walks down the aisle. A nice march or something with a beat to which the attendants can walk in rhythm works well. Traditional songs for the processional include: Fanfare by Couperin, Wedding March from Marriage of Figaro (Mozart), and, of course, Here Comes the Bride from Lohengrin (Wagner). Right before the bride and her escort (usually her father or another male family member) appear at the back of the wedding site, the music pauses and everybody rises to honor the bride. As she walks down the aisle, a new song is played; it is usually joyful, upbeat, and louder in volume than the previous songs.

Sometimes, a ceremony will have music softly playing while a prayer is being given or a poem is being recited. A musician might play or a soloist might sing at some point during the ceremony. Selections like Pachelbel's Canon in D Minor, Bach's Jesu, Joy of Man's Desiring, and Schubert's Ave Maria make beautiful ceremony music.

Finally, music fills the air during the recessional, as the wedding party walks back up the aisle. The music for the recessional is usually a quicker tempo than the processional. Popular recessional selections such as Handel's Postlude in G Major or the theme from his Water Music, and Beethoven's Ode to Joy offer upbeat and celebratory tunes as the wedding party and guests exit.

Sometimes a special musical group for a wedding fanfare is appropriate (bagpipes, trumpets, etc.).

Reception Music

For the reception, the music and the musicians help establish the overall mood. It might be a classical orchestra fashioned in black tuxedos and long gowns, a jazz band in dark sunglasses and hats, a rock n' roll band in torn jeans, or a deejay spinning a variety of CDs.

Whatever type of musicians you employ dictates the kind of dancing (if any) people will experience. For example, a swing band will have energetic couples swinging on the dance floor, and a country band will have folks line-dancing and two-stepping. An orchestra will promote waltzing, and upbeat rock n' roll CDs will have your guests boogying up a storm! If there is talent in the family, prevail upon them to perform—even if it is only one number. It can result in a warm memory enjoyed by many wedding guests.

322

Of course, what type of music you have playing at your wedding and reception also dictates how much money you will spend. Popular bands cost much more than up-and-coming bands. Deejays' fees also vary greatly. You can expect to spend at least $200 on music, and as much as $1,000 and more.

If you require that the musicians wear something specific (such as black suits and dresses), be up-front with your request. If they do not already have such costumes in their wardrobes, you might have to pay for their rentals.

Contracting with the Band

When interviewing musicians to perform at your reception, they should offer you an example of their work—usually in the form of a demo tape. Be certain to share this tape with those people directly involved with your wedding. Most people have strong feelings about what music is or is not appropriate for a wedding and it is better to resolve these issues quickly.

Sometimes, the band will invite you to peek in on a party for which they are playing. Ask if they have ever performed for a wedding; and if so, you can ask for references.

There will be a contract to sign—a practice you will become very familiar with before the planning of your wedding is finished. Read it in full, and pay attention to how long they will play at the reception, and other such details. The contract should spell out the fee charged for performing at a wedding. If a friend is performing, and he or she refuses to take payment, make certain you give them a nice gift for their effort and generosity. Payment can be rendered at the rehearsal unless another time is mutually agreed upon.

Musicians' Needs

Many musicians need special set ups for their equipment. Make certain you review with them their specific needs so that when they arrive, they do not experience any problems or surprises. For the ceremony musicians, make certain they attend and perform at the wedding rehearsal. At this time, any discrepancies between soloist and accompanist, or equipment needs and what the particular site offers, can be exposed and resolved. Also, make certain the musicians for the reception can set up close to the dance floor and double-check their equipment needs prior to the reception. This is particularly vital for outdoor sites where wiring for speakers and microphones must be provided. Be certain to prepare for protecting expensive sound equipment from inclement weather. Without careful planning, a slight breeze or an errant guest can push over an instrument or speaker and cause extensive damage.

Music Selections

Good musicians will keep the guests' attention and keep everyone entertained so they do not leave the reception too soon.

For both the ceremony musicians and the reception musicians, you will want to review what songs they will be playing. Some musicians perform at many weddings and have a repertoire of classics that are acceptable for virtually any wedding. If you have a special song you would like to have played, make certain the musicians know in plenty of time for them to practice.

Sometimes, if the song is very rare, the musicians might need you to provide them with the sheet music. If this is the case, you will want to have a back-up song in mind, just in case the music cannot be found or the musicians cannot play it well enough. Also, make certain there are enough copies of the music for each musician.

For the reception, you will want to request a special song for the bride and groom's first dance. This can be a song you listened to on your first date together, a song having words that capture your feelings for one another, the song the groom serenaded the bride with when he asked her to marry him, or any tune that you classify as "your song."

If music be the food of love, play on. . . .
—William Shakespeare

328

Chapter Eight: Getting Dressed

Dressing the Bride

Every bride wants to look beautiful on her wedding day, whether she has chosen a casual garden get-together or a lavish ceremony in a cathedral. She has been looking forward to this day for such a long time, and when it arrives, she puts all her insecurities and bashfulness aside—for this is her day to positively shine!

The Dress

The length, style, and elaborateness of a wedding gown depends upon the formality of the wedding, the time of day, religion, cultural traditions, and the season in which the wedding occurs, as well as the amount of money the bride can—and wants to—spend. Very basic gowns cost at least $100, and extravagant gowns can cost into the thousands.

Since the long, white gown and veil ensemble is best suited to a younger bride, older brides oftentimes wear lovely suits or cocktail dresses. They look just as pretty, only more sophisticated.

Many modern brides begin the wedding gown shopping process perusing through bridal magazines. There are a plethora of different magazines to choose from, and buying several of these magazines gives the bride more gowns to compare and contrast. Or, perhaps the bride saw a wedding gown during a wedding she attended, on television, or in a movie that caught her eye. Wedding fairs and festivals feature bridal-gown fashion shows, which can give the bride-to-be specific style ideas.

Some brides contrived an idea about what their wedding gown would look like when they were little girls, and that dream dress is precisely the one they want to wear.

The wedding gown has many components that contribute to its overall appearance and cost. There are many different silhouettes, skirts, collars, necklines, dress lengths, trains, and sleeves. Additionally, there is a plethora of fabric, beading, ribbon, and lace embellishment choices. And even within the family of white fabrics, there are many different shades from which to select.

If she wants to purchase a new gown, there are many bridal specialty shops and department stores that carry bridal gowns. Typically, there is an assortment of gowns on a rack in the store, and a salesperson can make recommendations about what style of gown would work nicely with the bride's body type, coloring, and wedding style.

The gowns on the rack in smaller bridal shops are typically larger in size, so a bride-to-be of almost any size can try the gown on in front of a mirror. Of course, the salesperson can tuck the dress back with her hands or special clips if the gown is too large. These dresses can then be altered or specially ordered. Bridal shops sometimes require an appointment, so it is best to check ahead of your visit.

A bride might choose to have her gown made by a professional seamstress, or someone she knows who is talented in this area. There are patterns available for purchase at sewing stores, or the bride might want to design her own. Having a dress made can save money or not—once again, depending on the elaborate details of the beading, lace, and fabric choices and the stitching and fitting labor involved.

If the bride is more cost-conscious and would like to wear a bridal gown that has been worn by other brides, she might consider looking in the local want ads, used clothing stores, or bridal shops which have such gowns available to rent. A vintage treasure might be out there, waiting for the perfect bride! Or, if her mother or grandmother's wedding gown is still in decent repair and it is a style and size that fits the bride, she can ask to borrow it. Most likely, her mother or grandmother will be honored to let her wear a wedding gown of theirs.

It is in good taste to select a wedding gown that is not too revealing, as the occasion of a wedding is a dignified one, indeed. Furthermore, she will want to choose a dress that her bridegroom would find attractive. If having a sanctuary wedding, the bride should check with the officiant to make sure her dress (namely color, sleeves, length, and neckline) abides by any set rules for modesty in the sacred ceremony. Also, the gown should be clean, pressed, altered to fit, and in its best repair before proceeding down the aisle.

When the bride removes the dress after the reception, she will want her mother, sister, or a girlfriend to hang the dress somewhere safe for her. Temporarily hanging the dress on a wooden hanger maintains its shape. Then, the bride will need to decide whether or not to have the dress dry cleaned, or dry cleaned and preserved. The latter can be expensive, but if the dress was costly or is an heirloom, it is worth the investment. Furthermore, if she suspects that her daughter or granddaughter will want to wear it someday, preserving it is important. Whatever you decide, do not leave your wedding dress in an ordinary plastic dry-cleaning bag. And if you can store it in a box, this is better than leaving it hung in a closet. Furthermore, store your wedding dress in a place that is protected from sunlight and humidity. Many of the more reputable dry-cleaning establishments offer special services for wedding gown preservation. They include special boxes treated to prevent yellowing of satins, silks, taffetas, and organzas.

The bride, for whatever reason, may decide not to preserve or keep her wedding dress. In this case, she may choose to sell or donate her gown to one of the many wedding dress rental businesses located in most sizable cities. Since a used wedding dress is usually only worth a fraction of the original purchase price, the bride needs to be prepared for the shock of letting her "dream gown" go for so little. In the end, she is really helping another bride experience a dream wedding of her own.

Formality of the Wedding Dress

Formality of Wedding	*Wedding Gown*
Very Formal	Floor-length, ornate gown with a cathedral- or chapel-length train
Formal	Floor-length gown with a chapel-length train
Semiformal	Floor-, ankle-, or knee-length gown, train optional
Informal	A nice suit, a cocktail dress, a simple gown, or just about anything the bride wishes to wear

White or Not White

Many cultures embrace colorful wedding attire for their brides. For example, red is the auspicious color of good fortune used for a multitude of Hindu, Islamic, and Chinese bridal gowns.

In many parts of the world, a bride wears a white dress on her wedding day. In the Victorian era, white cloth was precious and expensive, due to the repeated bleaching processes it underwent to reach the purest white. So, if a lady wore a pure white gown on her wedding day, it was a symbol of affluence as well as virginal purity.

Many believe white dresses should be reserved for virginal brides alone, as a white wedding gown symbolizes the bride's purity. In the past, any bride on her second marriage—or who had any kind of sexual relationship before her wedding night—

could not wear white. If she did, it was considered scandalous! Today, whether accepted or not, many women experience sexual intimacy before their wedding night, and if they want to wear a white gown, it is finally acceptable.

Other symbols of a bride's purity include: a veil, a myrtle or floral wreath worn on her head, wearing the hair down for her wedding, or carrying orange blossoms in her bouquet. On the other hand, if a virginal bride's hair color and skin tone looks more attractive in an off-white color, she can wear an off-white gown.

Nonvirginal brides wanting to adhere to this traditional school of thought can wear ivory, candlelight, or cream. Or, (especially for second marriages or very casual weddings) brides can wear any color at all, so long as it flatters her. She can wear pure white with colored accessories, for a variation.

In short, it is fine for any bride to wear any color and style of dress, no matter how many times she has been married. After all, it is supposed to be the dress of her dreams.

May the gods grant you all things
which your heart desires,
and may they give you a husband and a home
and gracious concord,
for there is nothing greater and better than this—
when a husband and wife
keep a household in oneness of mind,
a great woe to their enemies
and joy to their friends,
and win high renown.
    — Homer

Bridal Accessories

The perfect accessory makes a lovely companion to the bridal gown. When selecting accessories, the bride should have selected her gown, or even have it with her to make certain the styles, colors, lengths, and so forth, work well together. For instance, a bride typically does not want her veil to be longer than her gown, and a pure white gown adorned with diamond-like beads is mismatched with an off-white, pearl-beaded veil, or a large pearl necklace can appear to be heavy and cluttered when worn with a high-collared gown.

Veils and Headpieces

When selecting a veil—if the bride chooses to wear one—she should try it on, having a general or exact idea as to how she will wear her hair. *Note: If the bride has her hair done professionally before the wedding, she will need to have her headpiece and/or veil with her.* It is also important to try a veil on with the gown itself, giving an overall picture of how the gown or dress and veil complement one another.

There are easily as many variations in veil and headpiece styles as types of wedding gowns. Many brides decide to wear a veil, but some opt for a floral headpiece, hat, or none of these. A multilayered veil fastened to the head with an ornate tiara, a simply elegant white headband or bejeweled hair comb, a demure floral crown, feathers or beads and a cowboy hat with tiny flowers making up the hatband—all are among the varieties from which a bride may select. Her choices will be keyed to the theme of the wedding and how formal or informal it is.

Formality of Wedding	*Wedding Gown*
Very Formal	Full-length veil with decorative headpiece
Formal	Fingertip-length veil, decorative headpiece or hat
Semiformal	Shorter veil with shorter dress, fingertip-length with longer dress
Informal	Typically, no veil worn

Gloves

Usually reserved for the more formal weddings, gloves add an elegantly romantic accent to the bride's wedding ensemble.

Generally, the longest gloves, above the elbows or just below, are worn with sleeveless wedding gowns, while wrist-length gloves go well with long-sleeved wedding gowns.

Shoes

If the bride wears a floor-length wedding gown, it is feasible that no one will even see her shoes, except, perhaps, during the garter-removing ceremony. However, the bride's shoes are a very important player in the scheme of things, and they should be chosen wisely. The shoes, naturally, should match or blend nicely with the wedding gown, whether the gown is long or the dress is tea length or shorter. There are several considerations to make when shopping for wedding shoes.

- If the bride is taller than—or almost as tall as the groom, she might choose to wear flat or low-heeled shoes.

- If the wedding is outside on grass, pointy heels are difficult to walk in.

- Since the bride will be standing and dancing in her shoes, she will want them to be as comfortable as possible.

- If the soles are smooth and slick, textured patches should be adhered to the soles to lessen the possibility of slippage. A light scuffing with sandpaper is another option.

- The shoes should complement the wedding apparel, and therefore the formality of the wedding.

Since new shoes can cause problems, it is wise to break them in gently before the wedding day. The bride can wear them on carpeting around her home, before the wedding. She should wear the shoes during the wedding rehearsal.

Jewelry

Many brides wear necklaces, earrings, bracelets, rings, broaches, lockets, and other jewelry when they marry. With jewelry, it is best not to overdo. You do not want gargantuan diamond drop-earrings, for example, to detract from the wedding gown.

Pearls are always a good choice, as they look nice with almost any wedding gown. Many brides choose to wear heirloom jewelry, or a piece that has special meaning to them (such as a promise ring the groom gave her when they were first dating). And some brides do not wear any jewelry at all, supporting the "less is more" theory of simplicity.

Undergarments

What a bride wears underneath her wedding gown can determine whether the gown looks beautiful or less so. She wants her body to appear especially trim and smooth, and her gown to take on the shape for which it was designed. Therefore, wearing the proper slip, bra, hosiery, panties, and other lingerie pieces is imperative. A slip will be necessary if the gown or dress is not lined or heavy enough, as with bridal satin, to avoid see-through. The best way to make certain the undergarments do their jobs well is to actually try everything on together before the wedding.

In addition to making the gown look as nice as possible, the right undergarments can make the bride feel confident and sexy. A strapless, satin push-up bra emphasizes her breasts for this special day, perhaps as part of an exquisite matching bra-and-panty ensemble. Then, instead of traditional panty hose, she can wear thigh-high hose secured with a tantalizing, lacy garter belt.

A garter is another accessory worn underneath the wedding gown, and while it is not necessarily a functional piece, it is spotlighted in the wonderful tradition of "Removing the Garter," (see pages 421–422), performed by the groom at the reception. Also, its purpose is dual-fold when blue in color, for the garter can play the role of "something blue" in the delightful custom of the bride wearing: "Something old, something new, something borrowed, something blue."

Hairstyles

Many brides choose to have their hair done by a professional hairstylist for their wedding, while some brides feel more comfortable styling their own. Either way, it is recommended that the bride does not leave any major hair decisions to the last minute. She should already know how it will be styled, and she should have it styled the way she wishes a week before the wedding day to practice with her headpiece or veil. If she desires a special haircut, permanent, body wave, relaxing, coloring, or highlighting procedure, any of these should be done several weeks before the wedding. Another good recommendation is for the bride to keep her hair as healthy as possible prior to her wedding day—so wearing a swim cap while swimming, using a deep conditioner, (temporarily) eliminating damaging styling techniques, and so forth—can aid in the overall beauty of her hair on her wedding day.

350

Any hair accessories, such as a beaded hair comb or veil, should be used while styling the bride's hair the day of her wedding. Also, if the bridesmaids are to wear specific headpieces, they should bring the headpieces when they get their hair done (or use the headpiece while doing their own hair).

Makeup

Because the bride will have her photographs taken throughout her wedding day, she will want to wear makeup that will enhance her best features. Like her hair, she should "practice" applying makeup (if she wants to do it herself) or have a professional makeup artist apply cosmetics several days before the actual wedding date, so there are no surprises.

A bride might have a professional help her select the makeup colors and varieties that are most becoming for her coloring and the color(s) of her wedding apparel. Then, with her new cosmetics and her new makeup application savvy, she feels confident enhancing herself for her wedding.

The basic makeup products that a bride should use to look her best include:

- Foundation or base
- Eye shadow
- Eye liner
- Mascara—waterproof
- Blush
- Lipstick and lip liner
- Finishing powder

Makeup should be applied thoroughly enough to camouflage flaws (such as under-eye circles) and accentuate her prettiest features (such as her full, luscious lips), but should not be caked-on or unnatural looking. Using stay-put or waterproof products is beneficial, as a bride with "raccoon eyes" is sad indeed. Also, the bride should pack a few makeup products such as lipstick and powder or oil-removing papers for touch-ups throughout her wedding day.

Other things a bride can do before her wedding to look her best include having brows waxed. Indulging in a manicure and pedicure. Having a facial (a week or more preceding the wedding). Working out. Eating nutritious foods, drinking a lot of water. Be certain to not skip meals and get plenty of rest.

Brides with lighter complexions often make the mistake of working on a dark suntan for their wedding day. While a bronzed body might look beautiful in a bikini for a tropical island honeymoon, she will look better in all the photographs if not too tanned. Also, being in the sun or a tanning bed for extensive time periods might dry out or irritate her skin, making her face bumpy and scaly. An alternate route to tanning is to use self-tanning lotion.

If a bride decides to use a self-tanning lotion, she should familiarize herself with the product and follow the directions word-for-word, using it several weeks before the wedding to practice skillful application. Some salons and spas offer professional exfoliation and self-tanning lotion application, but it is still risky to try it for the first time right before the wedding day.

Dressing the Mothers

The mothers of the bride and groom will want to dress appropriately for the style and formality of the wedding. For a formal or semiformal affair, they will wear nice dresses or suits, at least knee-length. For a formal, evening affair, long gowns are in order. For an informal wedding, a pantsuit or business dress.

If the bride and groom's mothers wear dresses similar in style and color, the receiving line and wedding photographs will look harmonious. It is up to the bride's mother to determine the style of dress and relate this information to the groom's mother. They should not wear identical dresses, however. Nor should they wear dresses the same color as, or more formal than, what the bride wears. Both mothers traditionally wear corsages.

Dressing the Fathers

What the fathers wear is largely up to them, with helpful suggestions from the bride and groom. Generally speaking, they wear something similar to —or slightly less formal than—what the groom and groomsmen/ushers wear. If wearing tuxedos, both fathers should be dressed alike. This will help balance the wedding pictures and make a reception line look more harmonious. If the fathers have shoes that match the tuxedos, they may opt to wear them rather than the sometimes uncomfortable rented shoes.

At the most casual, they should wear something similar to what the other male guests will be wearing. Both fathers traditionally wear boutonnieres, as do the grandfathers.

Chapter Nine: Planning the Reception

The reception, which usually begins immediately following the wedding ceremony, is a celebration of the newlyweds. The reception can take place at home, in a traditional party setting, or in a creative and highly personalized place.

The Home Reception

Some couples choose to have their wedding reception in their home or in the home of the bride's parents. A reception in the home is intimate, cozy, and delightful. If there are less than twenty-five guests, it is feasible for the bride and her family to host the reception without the aid of professional planners and caterers. Preparing food ahead of time and keeping the celebration simple and intimate helps everything go smoothly.

Some believe having their wedding reception at home will cost less than renting a facility. However, if the yard and house need considerable improvement, then having a reception at home can still be very costly. Of course, once the improvements are made, those improvements remain even after the bride and groom leave for their honeymoon.

Traditional Reception Venues

Most couples choose to have their reception in a traditional location, such as a hotel ballroom, country club, or restaurant. If a traditional reception site or center is your choice, many have appropriate menus, music selections, and table arrangements already established for a wedding reception or large party. They will recommend florists for table enhancements or take care of them.

Usually, when you call a restaurant or hotel and mention you are looking for a place to hold your wedding reception, a representative will invite you in for a tour and to sample menu items. They typically charge "per head," meaning a certain price for each guest you expect. Some places differentiate between children and adults, but many do not. Additionally, you will likely pay a facility charge, parking attendant fee, bar costs, gratuities, and so forth. Read your contract in full, and ask questions if it includes something you do not understand or recognize. Some reception sites even include a wedding cake in their overall wedding package.

Nontraditional Reception Venues

Still other couples opt for more creative wedding and reception sites, like a sailboat, a ski lodge, a museum, a beach, a train station . . . the possibilities are endless! Sometimes, these types of places are built for receptions, or can easily accommodate a large party. However, if they are not, make a phone call or two to find out if something can be arranged. You might need to bring your own caterer, and the overall setup and cleanup might be your responsibility.

The Wedding Cake

A wedding reception just does not seem right unless there is a wedding cake for all to "Ooooh!" and "Ahhh!" over. Whether highly formal or quite casual, you will want to spotlight a wedding cake, a groom's cake, or even several beautiful and unique cakes for a large party of guests.

History of the Wedding Cake

Some historians claim that the tradition of the wedding cake is rooted in ancient Rome, where wheat and barley were crumbled over the bride's head, signifying fertility. A guest who ended up with a crumb would therefore have very good luck.

In the Middle Ages, wedding guests brought small sweet rolls and stacked them one on top of the other. The newlyweds who successfully kissed over the towering bread were sure to experience a long, loving married life together. At some point, frosting was spread on the rolls to help them stick together, aiding the couple in the success of their kiss.

Serving the Cake

If a meal is served at the reception, the cake is cut after the main course and served as part of dessert. If no meal is served, or if it is buffet style, the cake is cut and served right before the bride and groom change out of their wedding attire, or prior to the dance if they do not change clothing.

The rest of the pieces of cake are served by the wait staff, or by members of the family (if the wedding is smaller in size).

The Knife

For many weddings, the knife used to cut the cake is quite fancy. It might have a pearl or bejeweled handle, be antique silver, or have a pretty bow tied around its handle. It should be sparkling clean, thin, and sharp (or serrated). The knife might be paired with a plain silver cake server, or the two can be purchased as a matching set. They are often engraved with the wedding date.

Cutting the Cake

Insert the knife into the wedding cake, angling the point downwards and the handle upwards. Pull the knife toward you. Some icings are particularly

365

sticky, so if the knife sticks while slicing, simply dip it in a container of hot water or wipe down with a damp, clean cloth before slicing each piece.

Most wedding cakes are tiered, making them more difficult to cut. Usually, the bride and groom slice a piece of cake together from the bottom tier, and then someone else cuts the remainder of the cake, setting the top tier aside for the bride and groom to eat on their first wedding anniversary. Additionally, any cake toppers or other cake decorations should be kept for the bride and groom.

The easiest way to cut a tiered cake is to remove the tiers. Then, individual slices are cut starting with the bottom tier. Round cakes are best cut in wedges. Sheet cakes, often with individual roses or buds, are cut in squares or rectangular pieces.

Ordering and Delivery

Sometimes, you can order the cake from the restaurant or country club where your reception is held. If you order it from a bakery, local grocery store, or caterer, you will need to inquire if they will deliver the cake to your reception. Most specialty bakeries own a van equipped to deliver and set up wedding cakes. Furthermore, bakers oftentimes want to set up the cake themselves, ensuring it is done correctly.

If someone must pick up the cake, be certain the vehicle is big enough for the cake to fit easily; it is best to have someone sit beside the cake, to keep it as steady as possible during the ride.

Familiar Baker

Perhaps an experienced good friend or family member offers to make your wedding cake. It might not be quite as fancy as a bakery's, but it will be beautiful, delicious, and meaningful nonetheless. A bride should never bake her own cake, however, for this brings bad luck.

Appearance of the Cake

The cake should be displayed where the guests can easily see it before it is cut and served. Typically, a wedding cake is a light flavor such as vanilla or lemon, and it is frosted in white or a pastel color, perhaps to match the wedding colors. The size of the wedding cake is dependent upon the size of the reception—the more guests, the more tiers. Generally, each pound of cake feeds five people.

The cake can be created in any shape, but a multiple-tiered round cake is the most popular. Wedding cakes can be simple, with a few icing

flowers or romantically accented with fresh flowers or greenery. Some people choose to top the cake with a figurine of a wedding couple, bells, doves, etc. The most elaborate wedding cakes have working water fountains, and other such details. More creative cakes include a group of hatbox-like cakes, a gingerbread house cake, or large sugar cookies artistically frosted with little brides and grooms.

Do Not Eat

Since wedding cakes are so expensive and so fancy these days, it is a growing trend for the formal wedding cake to be looked at, but not eaten. Some "cakes" are even made with foam centers rather than cake so they can appear more uniform in shape. As a result, smaller cakes, cookies, or dessert pastries are served to the guests.

The Groom's Cake

The groom's cake is a well-loved tradition. While optional, it is still a very popular and charming addition to the reception. Having a groom's cake allots guests the choice between having a slice of the bride's cake, a slice of the groom's cake, or a slice of both!

Typically darker in color than the wedding cake, the groom's cake can be fruitcake, chocolate, or the groom's favorite flavor. The groom's cake is much smaller than the wedding cake, perhaps one layer, or a sheet cake, or made in a ring. It can be frosted a solid color with minimal decorations, or accented with flowers and greenery that match those on the wedding cake. For a personal touch, the cake can be decorated with a theme, such as the groom's favorite sport, hobby, his current occupation, or anything else that the groom likes.

The groom's cake is placed on a smaller table close to the wedding cake and refreshment table. The groom's cake can be ordered from the same bakery as the wedding cake, or a good friend or close relative of the bride and groom might offer to bake and decorate it.

Customarily, individual pieces of the groom's cake are wrapped in pretty white or silver boxes and ribbons, and sent home with the guests for tasty keepsakes. Single guests who put the groom's cake underneath their pillow that night will dream of who they are going to marry, superstitious folks claim.

Other Cake Traditions

Another tradition involves baking little charms or trinkets right into the wedding cake, and the guests who find a charm in their slice of cake get to keep it as a memento. A twist on this idea is a wedding cake with several colored ribbons sticking out of its icing. Each ribbon is attached to a charm (which was baked into the cake), and each single girlfriend of the bride ceremonially tugs on a ribbon to reveal her fate. A wedding ring charm is considered the prize, as the lady who ends up with it is the next to marry. The least-wanted charms to get, the thimble and the button, reveal that they will die old maids! Another bad omen is pulling the penny out, for that means she will be poor. A horseshoe, clover, and wishbone bestow good luck on the ladies.

Customarily, the top tier (or a small portion, if it is not a tier cake) of the wedding cake is wrapped in freezer paper, taped, and stored in the freezer for a full year. Then, on the couple's first wedding anniversary, they eat a piece of the cake for good luck. Many bakeries keep this tradition in mind and will give you special directions to ensure the cake is as edible as possible come your anniversary.

Catering

If more than twenty-five guests are expected, it is best to hire a professional caterer. Whenever hiring a caterer, ask for references and sample the menu items you are considering. You will need to obtain a contract, and read it in full before signing. Check all the itemized costs, and inquire whether gratuities and any applicable taxes are included in the total. If gratuity (also called a service charge by some) is not added on the bill, tip around fifteen- to twenty-percent, or whatever you usually tip servers at nice restaurants.

Other issues to consider before hiring a caterer are: how many servers will come, how the tables and chairs will be set up, what professional attire is to be worn, china or place settings to be used, whether additional charges will be incurred for overtime and setup, etc. The caterer will want an estimate of how many guests you expect, and you will want to give him or her a close count (based on your RSVP cards or calls) as soon as possible. Ask the caterer when he or she needs a guaranteed head count.

Reception Menu

An experienced caterer will undoubtedly have suggestions for menu selections. Also, many wedding planner books provide failproof, traditional wedding menu items.

You will want to personalize the menu somewhat. For instance, if the bride's absolute favorite food is chocolate-covered strawberries, she can add those to the menu, displaying them beside the wedding cake if she chooses.

You will also want to offer menu items to appease vegetarians, sugar-free items for diabetics, and items for young children, if applicable. Further, if red meat is on your menu, it is nice to add an alternate meat choice, such as a tasty fish or a poultry dish.

There does not need to be a vast spread of food at your wedding reception. Just select and prepare each food item with care, make certain each food is displayed beautifully, and be certain there is enough food to go around. You do not want the food to run out, leaving some guests hungry and the buffet table looking ravaged.

As for beverages, like the food menu, offer a variety. Hopefully, every guest will like at least one of the drink selections you have chosen. You need not provide every brand and type of wine, liquor, soda pop, tea, and coffee. However, a basic offering of those you choose to serve will suffice. At the minimum, (nonalcoholic) punch and ice water should be served. Again, provide enough drinks and ice so that no guest goes thirsty. As a hint, the spicier and saltier the food is, and the warmer the weather, the more your guests will drink.

Spice a dish with love and it pleases every palate.
— Plautus

Chapter Ten: The Ceremony

Guests will start filtering in about thirty minutes early, but at least one usher should be stationed at the entrance about forty-five minutes before the ceremony. The guests will be seated upon arrival, and will be able to listen to music while waiting for the processional.

The wedding party should arrive at the wedding site thirty minutes to an hour before the ceremony is to start. If they dressed and primped beforehand, less time will be needed, of course. If the bride dressed beforehand, she can show up moments before the ceremony begins. The bride and the bridesmaids usually have a dressing room or dressing area where they get ready. Some Jewish and Protestant brides entertain guests in this room before the wedding.

Sometimes, the parents of the bride and groom remain out-of-sight until their grand entry. However, the parents standing at the entrance, warmly greeting guests, is gaining acceptance and favor.

Parking for Guests

Ideally, there are enough parking places for all of your guests at the ceremony and reception sites. If not, you will want to plan ahead for shuttling guests from a parking lot where there is room for everybody to park to the ceremony and/or reception site.

You might choose to have valet services available for your wedding guests, especially if the wedding is rather large, or if the weather forecast is particularly inclement. Some cities offer professional car attendant services (look in the phone book or on the internet). Or, you might approach a local high school or college and inquire if a school club or athletic team would like to take this job to earn money for their organization. Also, guests or other acquaintances might offer to help park cars. Of course, it is imperative that whoever takes on the valet responsibility is a trustworthy person, as well as an experienced and careful driver.

Transportation to the Ceremony

For more formal weddings, the mother of the bride and some or all of the bridesmaids leave the house first, followed closely by the rest of the wedding party. The bride and her father (or escort) leave for the wedding last. Sometimes, a limousine is used, which alleviates the need for different automobiles. If an open carriage is available—lovely!

Wedding Programs

An optional, but nice, touch for a wedding is a printed wedding program. Not only does a program allow the guests to follow the wedding ceremony, it also gives them a nice keepsake. Most wedding programs are folded in half vertically, however some are folded in half horizontally, and some are not folded at all and may be rolled and tied with a ribbon matching the bridal colors.

A title is printed on the top of the program. It includes the names of the bride and groom, the day and date of the wedding, the time the ceremony commences, where the ceremony is held, and the city and state. Sometimes, the title begins with a more creative phrase or description, such as *Welcome to our Wedding*, *The Wedding Mass Uniting*, or *The Blessing and Celebration of Marriage*.

Ceremony Seating Arrangements

Make certain there are enough seats for everyone attending the wedding. If the guests took the time to R.S.V.P. or returned reply cards, you will have a good idea of how many people to expect.

If there are too many seats, section off those to be reserved for the wedding guests. That way, guests will not be scattered. Pretty ribbons, strings of beads, or flower arrangements are ways to section off desired rows. Friends and family of the groom typically sit on the right side of the aisle, while friends and family of the bride sit on the left side (as facing the front). In some Jewish weddings, this is opposite. If it becomes lopsided because the bride has more guests than the groom (or vice versa), the usher can politely ask certain guests to sit on the side having fewer occupants. Alter the seating plan as needed for the physically impaired.

The bride's parents sit in the first row on the left side. Grandparents, siblings, or extra-special guests sit next to the parents. Aunts, uncles, cousins, and other close relatives and friends sit in the second and third rows. The same is true for the groom's side. If the parents are divorced, the mother (and her husband or companion) sits in the first row and the father (and his wife or companion) sits in the second row. If they are friendly, it is appropriate for both parents (and their spouses or partners) to sit in the first row. If the parents have passed away or cannot attend, other close relatives take the first pew.

The Processional

After the ushers escort the guests to their seats—the mother-of-the-bride being seated last—the processional begins. At this time, an aisle runner is laid down, if one is being used. If the groomsmen are already at the altar, the bridesmaids walk in single file (usually the shortest to the tallest) ending with the maid/matron of honor. Next, the ring bearer and flower girl venture down the aisle, either as a pair or the flower girl follows the ring bearer. The music will pause as everybody stands to honor the bride. The bride, escorted by her father, walks down the aisle last.

Processional for Traditional Formal or Semiformal Wedding

(Altar)

Officiant

Best Man, Groom

Bridesmaid, Groomsman

Bridesmaid, Groomsman

Bridesmaid, Groomsman

(Bride's Family) Maid/Matron of Honor (Groom's Family)

Ring Bearer

Flower Girl

Bride, Father

Processional for a Traditional Jewish Wedding

Rabbi or Cantor

Best Man

Father, Groom, Mother

Maid/Matron of Honor

Bridesmaid, Bridesmaid

Flower Girl

Father, Bride, Mother

At the Altar

The officiant faces the guests at the altar, the bride stands to the left and the groom stands to the right. (Historical fact: The bride stood to the groom's left in Christian weddings so he could have access to his sword in case a rival suitor tried to steal the bride away!) The bride and groom face the officiant. Next to the bride stands the maid/matron of honor, then the flower girl and the bridesmaids. The best man stands to the groom's right side, then the ring bearer and the groomsmen. This is a very traditional arrangement of positions at the altar, and variations are abundant.

The Address

The sermon or homily that the clergy-person gives at a traditional religious wedding discusses the couple's decision to marry and what that means, as well as inspires guests to reflect on their personal relationships. Religious in nature, the readings, scriptures, stories, prayers, or chanting might be experienced at this time. Most clergy-persons have their own ideas about what should embody the address, but if you have something you would like mentioned or deliberately avoided, discuss this with the officiant during your pre-wedding meetings.

The Unity Candle

Candles have long played an important role in the wedding ceremony. Some weddings include a candle ceremony. Its significance is usually described in the wedding program or by the officiant as the bride and groom (and sometimes their families) perform the ritual.

A popular candle ritual involves a large, unlit candle, which sits between the bride and groom. Both the bride and groom hold lit candles and come together over the large candle to light it together, symbolizing unity. Sometimes, their parents participate as well, showing that with the union of their children, their families are also uniting.

The Vows

The wedding sharing of the vows is what everyone came to your wedding to see. That exchange of commitment is the epicenter of the entire wedding experience. The vows are promises to one another, for a lifetime.

Many couples decide to repeat the vows the clergy-member or other officiant recites. Others read their vows or recite memorized vows to one another without frequent prompting from the officiant. Some officiants have a general outline that they follow, but allow the bride and groom some reign

in deciding what is included in or is eliminated from their vows.

An example of a traditional Christian vow is below:

In the name of God, I, (name), take thee, (name of partner), to be my beloved (husband or wife), to have and to hold from this day forward, for better, for worse, for richer, for poorer, in sickness and in health, to love and to cherish, till death do us part.

Here is an example of how a traditional civil vow might be personalized:

My dear, (name of partner), I take you to be my lawfully wedded (husband or wife). I vow to love you and to cherish you for as long as we both shall live. Before these witnesses today, I chose you as the (man or woman) with whom I will the share rest of my life.

On the other hand, some couples opt to write and recite their own vows. This adds a personal element to the wedding ceremony, which can be both fulfilling and emotional for the couple, as well as the guests who are listening. Before composing your own vows, make certain that both you and your partner truly wish to do this. After all, it may be difficult to memorize and deliver these intimate words in front of your guests, especially if you are nervous (as most everyone is) or overly emotional.

You will also need to talk to the officiant to make certain your vows are suitable, particularly if you are getting married in a church, temple, or synagogue. It is a good idea to have your partner share his or her vows with you before the wedding, to make certain the vows from both sides are fairly similar in length and style.

The Ring Ceremony

The ring ceremony is usually integrated into the exchange of vows. The groom recites his vows and places the wedding band on his bride's finger and then the bride says her vows and places a wedding band on her bridegroom's finger. Sometimes, the words, "With this ring, I thee wed," or something similar to the passage below is given for the ring ceremony.

I give you, (name of partner), this ring
as a symbol of my endless love for you, and
as a promise to honor you with all that I am
and all that I shall become for my entire life.

The Kiss

After the bride and groom say their vows, it is customary for the groom to kiss the bride. This is a celebratory part of the ceremony, and some guests might clap or whistle while others may even giggle. The kiss symbolizes that the husband and wife take each other as their very own forevermore.

If the bride wears a veil, either the maid of honor or the groom lifts the veil. The groom then kisses his new bride. Some couples immerse themselves in a highly sensuous kiss; while for others, a simple peck suffices. If you are uncertain what kind of kiss will work for you in this instance when everybody—including your grandparents—watches so closely, consider a medium-length kiss. Most guests do not want to see a really passionate kiss, yet too puny a peck can be quite disappointing all-around.

The Recessional

The bride and groom are the first to walk back down the aisle after the officiant pronounces them husband and wife. Next, the flower girl and ring bearer go, either together or the ring bearer follows the flower girl. The best man then escorts the maid/matron of honor, followed by the bridesmaids and groomsmen, all paired together. Lastly, the officiant walks down the aisle.

Recessional for Traditional Formal or Semi-formal Wedding

Bridesmaid, Groomsman

Bridesmaid, Groomsman

Bridesmaid, Groomsman

Maid/Matron of Honor, Best Man

Flower Girl, Ring Bearer

Bride, Groom

Take Note

Different religions, cultures, and families have a vast array of traditions for the wedding ceremony's processional, positioning of the wedding party at the altar, and the recessional. Those described previously serve as a basis of simply getting the wedding party down the aisle, through the ceremony, and back again, in an orderly fashion. Research your cultural background and speak with current church leaders to determine what is appropriate in your circumstances.

Wedding Day Jitters

Many people go through what is known as the "wedding-day jitters." It might be because the bride or groom is simply exhausted and cannot think clearly. Or, it might be a case of stage fright, where the bride or groom is extremely nervous about standing in front of everybody and saying their vows.

If you are prone to anxiety or nervousness, or feel overwhelmingly stressed right before your wedding, someone might recommend taking a pill (to combat anxiety or sleeplessness), or even to drink a glass of wine (to calm your nerves). While these suggestions are most likely given with the sincere wish to help you, do not take any recommendation unless it is something you have experienced before, and you know exactly how it affects you.

Getting married is a highly emotional event in one's lifetime, and sometimes the bride and/or groom will become emotional while the officiant performs the ceremony. A few tears are expected.

Sometimes, the wedding-day jitters indicate something much more serious. It could be the terrible feeling that you are simply not ready to take the tremendous step of marriage—at all, or with that particular individual. Hopefully, you have explored and reexplored your feelings before your actual wedding day. However, if you feel in your heart that this union is wrong, and getting married on this day to this person would be a mistake, do not do it. If your parents and fiancé are not with you at the moment of your epiphany, ask someone to bring them to you. Tell them your feelings. Then, ask a parent to go to the front of the wedding site and announce that you are very sorry, but you have decided to cancel your wedding.

The Show Must Go On

Unforeseen problems arise in everyone's lives, and it is not impossible that you wake up to find the garden wedding of your dreams is drowning under a summer rainstorm. Weather is something you cannot control, and if you are having an outside wedding, it is best to be prepared for temperamental weather conditions.

Once everyone is at the wedding, it is best to keep everything running as smoothly as possible. Having several tents set up (or ready to be set up) or having an alternate (and close) indoor location is recommended for any planned outdoor wedding. Sometimes, the most memorable weddings are when something goes wrong, yet everything works out okay in the end. Everyone will try to make the day special for the couple.

Groom Seeing the Bride Before the Wedding

It is considered bad luck for the groom to see the bride immediately before the wedding ceremony. Some brides-to-be forbid the future groom to see her wedding gown at all, even in the boutique or on the hanger in her mother's closet. Those who adhere to this tradition delight in the fact that "the groom's breath is taken away" at the first sight of his bride walking down the aisle.

However, some decide to have wedding photographs taken before the wedding, when everyone is fresh and so the guests will not have to wait for photos to be taken between the wedding and the reception. If that is the case, the groom will indubitably see the bride in her bridal attire.

Other Superstitions

"Something old, something new, something borrowed, something blue." According to this old adage, the bride must wear something on her person from each category at her wedding to have a successful marriage. It is a custom that is easy to fulfill, and many a bride cascades down the aisle in her great-aunt's earrings, new shoes, her best friend's lipstick, and a blue satin garter (See The Garter, pages 421–422). The bride who puts a coin (especially a sixpence) in her shoe is destined to be very wealthy, and sugar in her glove means she will have a sweet marriage.

"Evil spirits" can be quite problematic for brides, according to ancient legends. There are several ways to protect the bride from barrages of these mischievous spirits, including disguising her in a veil and dressing the bridesmaids in similar gowns, so the spirits cannot tell which lady is the bride. After the ceremony, guests throw rice to keep the evil spirits busy eating while the bride and groom slip into their getaway car. Their car is equipped with tin cans that dangle from the bumper, banging against the road to ward off the most persistent evil spirits! On their wedding night, the groom lifts the bride and carries her over the threshold, which is believed to keep demon spirits out of their new home and therefore invite good luck. Another take on this superstition, starting with the ancient Romans, is that if the bride trips or stumbles while entering her new home, the couple will have very bad luck. Furthermore, the bride should not enter the home on her own free will, because this shows that she is giving her virginity to her new husband too easily.

Each culture has its own treasury of wedding superstitions, and if you would like to participate for traditions sake, do so. However, just because it rains on your wedding day, do not automatically assume your marriage will be flooded with tears. There are countless numbers of soggy brides and grooms who are still happily married.

Cultural Customs

There are so many wedding customs you might want to integrate any one or a number of these rituals into your wedding. This is especially meaningful when the bride and groom come from different ethnicities.

Binding the hands of the bride and groom together, or "tying the knot," is a custom found in numerous faiths and parts of the world. Long ago, knots were believed to protect mortals from evil spirits. One such ritual starts with the couple casting a spell on one another, with a colorful ribbon binding their hands. Afterwards, they have to remove the ribbon without untying it, which designates that their marriage will be long-lived. Some South American cultures hang a long scarf over the couple's hands to symbolize union.

There are many food rituals that play a part in certain cultural weddings. Different types of food or food groups symbolize certain things. For example, bread is a symbol for life. The chosen foods can be served as nourishment as well as used in rituals that convey blessings and favorable attributes on the bride and her groom. One food ritual that is popular world-round is sharing a drink, such as wine, from a special cup.

A delightful custom found deep in African American roots is jumping the broom. The broom is used to sweep a circle clean, and then the broom is laid down or held horizontally on the East (the direction of beginnings) side of the couple. They say their wedding vows, hold hands, and leap over the broom together. Or, sometimes, they leap one after the other. The broom symbolizes making a clean sweep together in a binding act. It is a symbolic act of the covenant for the future, not just a "clean sweep" of the past. Seeing a white horse on your wedding day means your union has been blessed.

Water, fire, and other natural elements can be used in wedding ceremonies that symbolize particular changes. For example, water symbolizes purification, and couples oftentimes have a bowl of water on the altar for washing their hands or faces, signifying a fresh start. Or, blessed water of different temperatures can be dripped over the wedding rings as a way of blessing them. Fire can symbolize riddance of past ways, and a Native American tradition involves a fire into which everybody (including the couple) tosses artifacts symbolizing things they want to be freed from or have forgotten. Candlelighting ceremonies have graced many weddings worldwide. A symbol of undying love, divinity, and inspiration, the guests can hold candles and the flame passed throughout the rows for a beautiful ending to a wedding ceremony. Or, another well-loved ritual is when the bride and groom (and sometimes their parents) light a common candle (called a unity candle) with their individual candles—a symbol of becoming one.

412

Chapter Eleven: The Reception

The reception is a joyful affair to celebrate the bride and groom's new life together as husband and wife. It can be any level of formality, from very casual and intimate to rather large and highly extravagant. It might have a theme, such as "Under the Sea," "Black and White," or "Country Western." The bride and groom will want to capture their individual styles and personalities in their reception. However, formal weddings always call for formal receptions and informal weddings usually pair best with more relaxed, casual receptions.

A reception is almost always held immediately after the wedding ceremony, or at least right after the wedding party and family photographs are taken. If there is an unavoidably lengthy gap between the wedding and the reception, it should be noted in the invitations so guests can plan accordingly. Remember, the reception is to celebrate the newlyweds, so until they arrive, there is an awkward void, along with the anticipation.

Reception Sites

A reception can take place in the same building the wedding occurred. This is especially fitting if the wedding is in a church and the church has a nice reception hall, or if the wedding is in a hotel chapel and a ballroom down the hall is available. Or, the reception might be held somewhere entirely removed from where the wedding took place. If this is the case, do not pick a place that is too far from the wedding. A twenty-minute drive between the two is acceptable, but a two-hour drive is not. If your heart is set on a romantic restaurant where the two of you had your first date, but you do not really care which church your actual wedding takes place in, consider using a church near to that restaurant.

Multiple Receptions

Sometimes, there are multiple receptions held for a bride and groom, especially if one lives in a different state or country. Not all family members and friends can attend a long-distance wedding, so it is appropriate to have a reception somewhere that is more convenient for these special people. In this case, it is probable that a reception—either small or large—occurs immediately following the wedding. At a later date (perhaps on the way to or after the honeymoon), a second reception takes place in a different state or country. It is customary for the families in each place to assist with planning and expenses.

Transportation to the Reception

If the reception is held somewhere different than where the ceremony takes place, the bride and groom leave the ceremony site first. Then, the parents of the wedding couple leave, followed closely by the wedding party.

The bride and groom might want to arrange extraordinary transportation for the trip, such as a limousine, convertible or sports car, an old-fashioned car, a horse-drawn buggy, a motorcycle, or whatever means they choose.

Sometimes, transportation is arranged for all of the guests, as well. A very fancy wedding might transport the guests from the ceremony site to the reception (and back again) in limousines. Or, for a more casual wedding, a double-decker bus is a memorable and practical option.

The Receiving Line

The receiving line can consist of the bride and groom alone, or with their parents and the wedding party. The guests shake hands, hug, kiss, and extend warm wishes to the couple (and to any others in the line). The receiving line can take place immediately outside the room where the wedding ceremony is performed, as part of the recessional. Or, it can be formed in a prominent place wherever the reception is held. It is best to form the receiving line in an area where guest-traffic congestion is not a problem. Some couples elect to omit the receiving line, choosing instead to mingle with the guests informally. If that is the case for you, make yourself readily available to all of your guests.

Toasts and Roasts

The best man is traditionally the first to offer a toast to the bride and groom. A delicate tapping of a spoon or fork on a champagne glass signifies that he is about to speak, and the guests should stop talking. Once it is quiet enough for the best man to be heard, he stands and delivers a toast. After the bride, groom, and their guests acknowledge the best man's toast, the floor is open for anyone else wishing to toast the newlyweds. Some families and religions do not drink alcohol, and it is likely alcohol will not be served. In this case, it is fine to make a toast with whatever beverage is available, even if it is water.

A toast can be short and sweet, lengthy and eloquent, silly, sophisticated, or just about anything the toastmaster of the moment wishes to convey. It might be advice, a joke or funny story, a quotation, a poem, or anything deemed fitting. The important thing is sincerity. (Refer to *The Little Giant Encyclopedia of Wedding Toasts*, by Katherine Young, for ideas.)

Occasionally, a toast or series of toasts can avalanche into a full-fledged roast, with the bride or groom as the subject of this questionable style of humor. In certain circumstances this can be appropriate to a tasteful extent. The person making a toast should not in any way abuse the trust of the newlyweds or offend anyone whether they are in attendance or not.

Dancing

Many cultures embrace dancing as an embodiment of joyous celebration. Most receptions have some style of dancing, whether waltzing to a string quartet or boogying to a deejay.

Many cultures have special dances, such as the *hora*, which is an important part of the Jewish wedding. The *tarantella* celebrates Italian newlyweds, and the *Kaslamantiano* (or Circle Dance) celebrates Greek marriages. Some religions do not condone dancing, and sometimes the bride and groom simply do not enjoy dancing. In such cases, dancing should not be incorporated into the celebration.

It is customary for the bride and groom to dance the first dance, which symbolizes starting their new life together. The first dance is usually to a special song they selected beforehand. Customarily, the first dance is a waltz, but what kind of dance they choose is truly up to the newlyweds. When the next song starts, the bride's father cuts in and dances with the bride. Then, the groom asks the bride's mother to dance. Next, the groom's father cuts in and dances with his new daughter-in-law, and the groom's mother dances with the groom. After the groom and the fathers of the bride and groom dance with the bride and the mothers, the dancing continues with the guests participating.

In some areas, it is customary for the guests to pay the groom and bride a dollar for a dance. This is called "The Dollar Dance." The bills are pinned to the bridal couple's clothing, or simply stuffed wherever they will stick on the bride and groom's attire. Sometimes, the bride carries a small purse on her arm and guests put their dollars there.

The Garter

A fun and flirtatious tradition is the "Removing of the Garter." The bride wears a garter around her thigh underneath her wedding dress. The groom slyly removes the garter from her thigh insinuating that their marriage will be consummated later on that evening.

This event can be encouraged with funky music playing in the background, the groom removing the garter slowly and sexily, using his teeth, and so forth. Sometimes, the garter is tossed up to a group of single men, and whoever catches it is destined to be the next man to marry.

The Cake Ceremony

Before the cake is cut and served, it is customary for the bride and groom to perform the "Cake Ceremony." The groom's hand on top of the bride's, they cut the first piece together, from the bottom-most tier. Then, they feed each other a bite or piece of the cake, signifying that they will share their lives with one another. The groom can feed the bride first, or they can feed each other together (which is more fun). If they feed each other nicely, it indicates a nice marriage. If they feed each other playfully, it indicates a playful marriage. And if they smear the cake all over each other—well, you get the idea!

The Bouquet Toss

Tossing the bouquet is a much practiced tradition. The deejay or someone with a microphone or loud voice announces that the bouquet toss is about to commence, and asks that all single ladies please come forward. Sometimes, especially in large wedding receptions, the bouquet toss includes only the unmarried bridesmaids.

Then, the bride turns her back to the ladies and tosses her bouquet behind her. The bouquet might be an alternate one, so she may keep the one she carried in the wedding ceremony. Because the lady who catches the bouquet will be the next bride, sometimes the ladies go to extremes to end up with the bouquet. This can be quite humorous, and it is a definite photo opportunity! These candids will have photo album space.

Pranks

There is a reason couples try to keep the location of their wedding night a secret. If certain stealthy people (usually good buddies and kinfolks) discover where the couple will be staying, they might break in beforehand to create booby traps and pranks. Some of these include short-sheeting the bed (so the sheets look fine upon first inspection but are folded such that they only cover a portion of the people's legs), putting the wrong room number above the door, slipping funny and embarrassing items into the closet or drawers, and so forth.

Some pranksters "decorate" the newlyweds' get-away vehicle with shaving cream, balloons, signs, streamers, and tie old shoes and/or aluminum cans to the bumper. This might inspire the bride and groom to use an undisclosed vehicle, especially if

426

they are nervous that the pranksters could cause damage or costly, time-consuming cleanup.

Making pranks can be considered "fun" by some, but hopefully those who do so at your wedding keep it safe, undamaging, and within the guidelines of what you feel is appropriate. If your mischievous friends or relatives do perform a prank or two on your wedding day, no matter how annoyed you truly might feel, try to convey a good sense of humor. There is no reason to turn such behavior into an uncomfortable situation.

Drinking

Some wedding receptions do not offer alcoholic drinks, whether due to religious, moral, or financial constraints. If you decide not to offer alcohol, keep in mind that some guests might find a way to bring their own alcohol into the reception, or they might wander off to a nearby bar to have a quick cocktail. Even if you have strong feelings about alcohol, do not let their behavior bother you. They probably do not mean any disrespect to you, your family, or your religion. However, the majority of weddings in many cultures worldwide do offer alcoholic beverages to their guests.

Drinking can be a hazard in any event. People too young to legally drink alcohol might not be noticed drinking during a wedding reception. Those who lose control might drink too much and end up endangering themselves as well as other people. As with any event where you are responsible for providing alcohol, you must take precautions. Make certain anyone who has consumed too much alcohol gets a safe ride home or to their hotel. Designate a responsible person or group of people to be prepared to intervene with appropriate help, if necessary.

If there is an open bar at a wedding, this means that the guests are free to order as many beverages as they desire with no charge to them, except for a courteous tip to the bartender or cocktail server. If there is a cash bar, the guests are expected to pay for their alcoholic beverages.

The debate between whether to have an open bar or a cash bar is ongoing. To decide, ask yourself if you would have houseguests pay for their own alcohol—probably not. Therefore, having an open bar—albeit the more expensive route—is the best etiquette.

If you decide to have an open bar, it is acceptable to serve only beer, wine, champagne (for the toasts),

430

and nonalcoholic beverages. Or, if you still wish to have hard liquor (such as vodka, whiskey, tequila, etc.) served at an open bar, you can request the bartender uses "well" (not overly expensive) varieties in lieu of the top-shelf (very costly) varieties, unless a guest specifically requests a certain variety. For some affluent wedding planners, nothing but the best will be available. If you are purchasing your own alcohol for the reception, ask the liquor store manager if the store offers discounts for mass quantities and will take back unopened bottles. These are acceptable ways to make certain your bar tab does not run amuck. Many reception sites already have bar menus and procedures in place for large affairs, so make certain you discuss this issue with the appropriate personnel before the wedding to side-step possible confusion.

Smoking

If guests begin smoking cigarettes or cigars in an enclosed reception hall, have someone who has been preassigned to kindly ask them to refrain from smoking.

Seating at the Reception

The issue of seating is considered during the initial wedding planning. Formal and semiformal receptions usually have a bridal table, where the bride, groom, their attendants, and (if space allows) spouses and guests of the attendants sit. The parents' table includes the bride's parents, the groom's parents, the officiant and his or her spouse, as well as grandparents, godparents, and close relatives, as seating space allows.

For a formal wedding with a seated dinner, place cards might be used to indicate who sits in which seat. Typically, tables are put together with guests who are close in age and who know each other or would enjoy each other's company upon introduction. Those who bring dates, spouses, or young children should be seated beside each other whenever possible.

Guests who do not get along (such as divorced people) or would not get along very well (a staunch right-wing politician with an outspoken liberal, for instance) should not be seated together, if at all possible.

If place cards are used and the wedding is rather large, it is beneficial to have a reception greeter stand at the entryway, helping guests find their respective seats. Tables can be numbered or theme named and seating cards for them can be enclosed with the reception invitation.

Additionally, filling out the place cards is one task best left to the few days preceding the wedding, in case people have last-minute conflicts and are therefore unable to attend. The names should be written in black or another dark color ink. When using only first names might cause confusion, you can add their last names. For a very formal reception, titles and full names are used, i.e., Mrs. Charles Chi.

Gifts

Gifts from the Bridal Couple

It has become customary for the bride and groom to give a small token of appreciation to each and every guest who has taken the time, expense, and effort to attend. The favor might be a small, framed photo of the bride and groom, a candle, a box of chocolates, a flower, or any other memento of the occasion. If children come, it might be a good idea to furnish them with a small plaything to keep them busy and happy while the adults dance and mingle. However, giving gifts to the guests is strictly optional.

Gifts Brought by Guests

Many guests will bring wedding gifts to the reception. You will need a table set up in a prominent place near the entrance to hold the gifts. Formal receptions call for a gift attendant or two. This is an ideal opportunity to give a pair of teens, who love an excuse to dress up, a prominent role to play. The two people might also be a married or engaged couple. It is more pleasant for these valuable volunteers to have a companion to chat with while they keep order with gift cards and secure the safety of expensive gifts. If you do not designate a gift-table attendant for the reception, label the table with a sign. The sign can read simply, "Gift Table," or "Gifts for Tiffany and Glen," or something more creative, like a quotation.

Gifts Received

Sometimes, a table or area at the reception is dedicated to the display of gifts the bride and groom have received before the wedding day. This is a lovely way to show your appreciation, especially for gifts such as handmade quilts and heirloom furnishings.

Whether or not the gift card (showing who the gift is from) is displayed alongside the gift is up to you. Some people find this inappropriate, while others (notably the guests who gave the gifts) like the idea.

Opening Gifts

Wedding presents should not be opened at the reception unless it is a very small and intimate affair. It is best to open the gifts at a later date, whether with just the bride and groom in their private home, or with close friends and family members who wish to share in the experience.

Remember, the greatest gift is not found in a store nor under a tree, but in the hearts of true friends.
— Cindy Lew

Throwing Rice, Birdseed, Etc.

Throwing rice as the newlyweds leave their wedding together is a tradition with several meanings. Throwing rice is a way to keep the evil spirits occupied (eating) as the bride and her groom escape unharmed. Or, in times when large families equaled prosperity, the ancients believed tossing rice at the couple would ensure high fertility and therefore many children to work the land. Showering the newlyweds with fond wishes for their future happiness and prosperity never goes out of style.

Today, the rice-throwing tradition is still very popular. Some wedding/reception sites request alternate substances, such as birdseed, herb leaves, biodegradable paper confetti, or flower petals. Then again, some places—especially those with grassy fronts—do not allow birdseed, as it is prone to sprout pesky weeds. They have been known to suggest grass seed. Still others have the guests blow bubbles as the newlyweds flee for their honeymoon. Check with the wedding/reception site to see what its rules state.

If rice, birdseed, or rose petals to be thrown by guests is something you will incorporate into your getaway, consider having small bags handed to all guests who wish to participate. Some people use pretty paper or cellophane bags. Others use beautiful mesh bags that the guests can take home as a keepsake. They may be stamped with the bride and groom's initials and wedding date, tied with pretty ribbons, or embellished with tiny silk flowers or beads.

The thing that counts most in the pursuit of happiness is choosing the right traveling companion.

— Adrian Anderson

Chapter Twelve: Weddings Around the World

People of all ethnicities, all around the world, practice many interesting and charming wedding customs and rituals. Below find a small sampling.

Arabic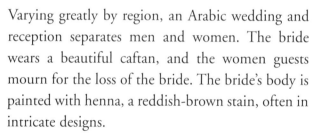

Varying greatly by region, an Arabic wedding and reception separates men and women. The bride wears a beautiful caftan, and the women guests mourn for the loss of the bride. The bride's body is painted with henna, a reddish-brown stain, often in intricate designs.

Chinese

In China, there is a very detail-oriented, time-consuming, and beautiful preparation process the wedding couple goes through before their wedding.

The bride symbolically mourns the loss of her family and friends and methodically moves her belongings into her new home. The groom brings several gifts to his wife's family which shows his respect and gratefulness to the family for allowing him to marry their daughter. Finally he must "bribe" the bridesmaids to allow him to enter the house and take his new bride.

The actual wedding ceremony is quite simple. The bride and groom go to an altar to show reverence and thanksgiving to their ancestors, *Tsao-Chün*, Earth, and Heaven. The groom's parents sip a ritual cup of tea, usually containing lotus seeds or dates. The bride and groom bow to each other, showing great respect. In some parts of China, the couple shares a mixture of wine and honey from a single goblet (or two goblets bound together with red string), and then they consume their wedding dinner together. During the reception, it is expected the bride will make several changes of beautiful wedding robes or gowns.

The colors red and gold symbolize happiness and wealth, so these colors are weaved into many aspects of the Chinese wedding, including the envelopes of the wedding invitations, the bride's wedding dress, candles, and envelopes of gift money.

Cuban

Weddings in Cuban communities are grand celebrations, complete with music and dancing. A variation of the "dollar dance," where guests pin money to the bride's dress and veil, is almost always a part of the reception. The guests all bring the couple a gift, and the bridal couple sends their guests home with gifts from them.

Czech

Fertility is given great weight in a Czech wedding, and before the ceremony even begins, an infant is laid on the wedding bed to promote fertility. The bridesmaids pin the herb rosemary on the guests, hoping to bestow luck and fertility upon the bride and groom.

Dutch

In Holland, the family hosts an elaborate party for the wedding couple. Hearty food dishes include pickled fruits and vegetables signifying long life to the prosperous couple. Cheese is a given in many beautiful hors d'ouevres. The bride and groom perch underneath evergreens, which symbolizes unending love. The bride and groom plant lily-of-the-valley in their home garden, and when it blooms again every year, they renew their love for one another.

English

For good luck, the bride carries a horseshoe decorated with streamers on her arm. Flower girls scatter flower petals on the aisle before the bride, which symbolizes a happy life. After the wedding, church bells ring, spreading the happy news throughout the land. A fruitcake is the English wedding cake of choice, and the top layer is saved for the couple's first child's christening. (The fruitcake layer is wrapped in a cloth soaked in brandy and placed it in a tin to keep it as fresh as possible for as long as possible.)

Filipino

During a Filipino wedding, the bride and groom release a pair of doves from a flower-decorated bell, which symbolizes everlasting love. There is much dancing and celebrating, and a variation of the "dollar dance" is usually performed. Dishes of colorful foods in quantities to feed streams of family and friends are generously provided. Family participation is of utmost importance.

French
For good luck, wedding guests throw laurel leaves as the wedding couple exits the church and heads for their reception. At the reception, the bride and groom share wine out of a silver cup that has been used in weddings from many former generations. After the reception, the couple might have to tolerate prankster friends who make jokes and commotion outside their bridal chamber until the groom invites them in for food and drink.

German
A German wedding celebration spans several days. First, the couple visits the city to partake in a civil wedding with close friends and family. Then,

everyone eats dinner together. The next day, friends host a big party, or polterabend, to celebrate the occasion. Many plates and other breakables are smashed as a sign of good luck. The third day, the couple has a traditional religious wedding ceremony, where they hold decorative candles. A reception follows. When the bride and groom try to escape the reception, their friends might provide obstacles and the groom must promise something, usually a party, gifts, or money), in order to "get out" safely with his bride.

Greek

The best man or groom's godfather crowns the wedding couple, symbolizing that they are the king and queen of the celebration. The threesome walks around the altar three times. Sugarcoated almonds are given to all guests, showing the bitter-sweetness of the marriage relationship. Line dancing, with everyone participating, can take the reception to breakfast the next morning.

Indian

In India, the bride wears a beautiful, traditional silk sari. Her hands and feet are painted with henna dye in beautiful patterns with symbolic significance. The brothers of the groom toss flower petals at the couple to protect the bride and groom from evil and to wish them a beautiful life together.

Irish

Traditionally, a wedding in Ireland whether Roman Catholic or Protestant, is followed by a rambunctious reception complete with silly toasts, drinking, music, and dancing. It may go on for a day or two. The "jaunting char" is a customary dance where the groom is carried around the mob of guests in a chair. A liquor-laced fruitcake is a favorite wedding cake. Family members of all ages participate.

May your heart be warm and happy, with the lilt of Irish laughter. Every day in every way, and forever and ever after.

— Irish toast

Italian Roman Catholic
After the wedding Mass, the newlyweds wander through the town square greeting neighbors. The villagers set up a log, hand the couple a double-handled saw, and they proceed to saw the log in half, working together. This action symbolizes the need to work together for the remainder of their married lives. The guests throw sugarcoated almonds at the newlyweds, symbolizing the bitter-sweetness of life's journey.

Japanese

In Japanese ceremonies, a bride wears the traditionally beautiful and feminine kimono and a white headpiece—a hood to hide her horns of jealousy. Her hair is elaborately styled and lacquered and her makeup is often stylized. The bride and groom become husband and wife when they take nine consecutive sips of sake (rice wine). Japanese elders deliver speeches and make toasts to the newlyweds which can go on for hours. The guests enjoy a feast of fish, rice, and sake. Japanese weddings are lavish indeed, and even middle-class families have been known to spend outrageous amounts of money for their children's weddings.

Korean

The Korean bride wears a colorful gown with white sleeves. Her cheeks bear circles of red to ward off evil spirits. The groom introduces his bride to his parents, at which time the groom's father tosses red dates to the bride, showing his desire for numerous healthy grandchildren.

Latin American

The ring bearer and flower girl are dressed like a miniature groom and bride. The father of the bride holds a plate full of coins covered with a cloth that symbolizes the bride's dowry.

Lithuanian

So that the bride and groom never live in hunger, they receive bread at their reception. They also eat honey and wine at their reception, so that they will have a very good life together.

Mexican

Before the wedding, the bride's and groom's parents bless them in their home. The groom gives his bride thirteen gold coins to show he will support her. A small chest of coins, called arras, is an integral part of the wedding ceremony, as it symbolizes wealth and strength. The godparents of the bridal couple are honored guests.

Moravian

A wonderful ritual in Moravian weddings consists of the bride and groom lighting a large candle together. Then, the flame is passed throughout the guests, who all hold beeswax candles. Soon, the entire wedding is aglow with the warmth of friends and family, united in the bond the bride and groom have expressed.

Native American

Marriage customs among Native Americans are varied and beautiful. Southwestern Native American wedding couples eat corn hash made from yellow and white corn, mixed together. Yellow symbolizes woman and white symbolizes man, so as they eat, it shows the coming together of the two sexes. They wash their hands during the ceremony, therefore washing away evil and past loves. The bride's dress is colorful, and each color symbolizes a different direction of the Earth to be honored.

Many tribal customs require a payment from the groom to the bride's family for her hand in marriage. An interesting twist practiced by Northern California tribes is the full versus half-marriage custom. If the groom could not pay a "respectable" price for his intended, or if the bride's family had need of more men in the clan, a half price could be paid and the man would remain a member of the bride's family. A full payment would result in a full-marriage and the bride would become a member of the groom's family.

In many eastern tribes, the bride and groom select four sponsors who give spiritual and marital guidance throughout the ceremony. These sponsors also commit to helping the couple adjust to marriage. In their ceremony, the bride and groom make their commitments to the Creator and so there is no breaking of such a union. In many Native American wedding celebrations, the bride and groom give a gift to each person attending the festivities.

Polish

Before her wedding, the bride's girlfriends undo her traditional braids. Then, Polish youngsters stand in the street, blocking the wedding party from getting to the wedding. The best man customarily pays the children off, and therefore saves the day. The parents of the bride and groom give them bread (which represents success) and salt (which represents bitterness). Guests give the bride gifts of money. The bride ties a decorated apron with big pockets around her waist, to hold the gifts of money she receives. Polish wedding receptions are notorious for their exuberant drinking, dancing, and general merry making, often for several days.

Puerto Rican

The priest blesses the arras (a plate filled with coins) and hands it to the groom. The groom then offers the arras to his bride, who treasures it, assuring they will have good fortune. At the reception, a variation of the "Dollar Dance" is performed, with guests pinning money to the bride's attire. As favors, guests take special pins with the bride and groom's names on them, which are called capias, from a doll that looks similar to the bride.

Russian

Right before her wedding, a Russian bride asks her parents to forgive her for her mistakes, and they offer her bread and salt so she will never suffer from hunger. At the reception, loved ones make toasts and the guests join the wedding couple in sipping champagne. The champagne glasses are thrown on the floor, and if they break, this suggests that the couple will have a joyous future together. Interestingly, if the bride and groom desire a girl for their firstborn, they display a doll on the front of their get-away car; and if they wish for a boy first, they display a bear on their car.

Russian Orthodox weddings go on for hours in a Byzantine-style church where framed icons of Mary are carried. During the long ceremony of blessings, the bride and groom wear crowns that are so heavy their attendants must assist in holding them.

Beautiful chanting by the priests makes the sacredness of the ceremony abundantly clear.

Scandinavian

A parade of musicians makes its way to the wedding ceremony. The bride wears a crown, which represents her innocence. Birch branches decorate the inside of the church, and the bride and groom are covered with a cloth to keep them safe from evil.

Scottish

Scottish tradition requires the groom to don a kilt, and the bride is resplendent in a beautiful white gown. Bagpipe music is a must and may be heard throughout a Scottish wedding and reception.

Some of the more common Scottish wedding traditions include the washing of the bride's feet, the "first foot," the cutting of a ribbon, the scramble or scrammy, and the tossing of the blue garter.

In washing the bride's feet, a married lady's wedding ring is placed in a pan of water and as unmarried women wash the bride's feet in preparation for her wedding, they search the pan trying to be the first to find the ring. The lucky lady who finds the ring is suppose to marry next.

The "first foot" is the first person encountered by the bride on her way to the wedding ceremony. The bride is suppose to give this person a coin and a drink of whisky.

After the ceremony, the bride's father may cut a ribbon stretched across the church gate, symbolizing cutting his daughter free.

When exiting the church, the newly married groom may scatter coins for the children attending the wedding to ensure good fortune for the marriage. As might be expected, this causes a "scramble" or "scrammy" among the children.

At the wedding reception, the groom often removes a blue garter from the bride's leg and tosses it toward a group of bachelors. He who catches the garter is suppose to be the next one married.

Vietnamese

The groom leads a parade, picking up friends and family along the way to his bride's house. Her mother does not join, as it would insinuate competitiveness. The friends and family present the bride with wonderful gifts.

Chapter Thirteen: Canceling or Postponing the Wedding

Unfortunately, weddings sometimes need to be canceled or postponed. The weather, a death in the immediate family, an ill or injured bride or groom, or a last-minute decision not to marry after all—these are all factors that can lead to a cancellation or postponement.

Notification by Mail

If there is time, especially if a formal wedding must be canceled or postponed, it is best to send notices by mail to all invited guests as soon as possible. Formal note cards, in the same style as the invitations themselves, work well. Or, if there is not enough time to have special cards printed, you can send other cards, either printed or handwritten.

Below is an example of how a card for a canceled wedding might be worded:

> *Mr. and Mrs. Paul Dickson*
> *announce that the marriage of*
> *their daughter*
> *Elizabeth May*
> *to George Clark*
> *will not take place*

If you must change or postpone the date of your wedding, it is most preferable to insert a printed card stating that the date of the wedding has changed (and what that new date is) into the invitation. If the invitations have gone out already, cards with the new information must be sent as soon as possible.

Notification by Phone

Phone calls, especially if the cancellation or postponement occurs shortly before the wedding date, are also acceptable. If desired, the bride and her mother might enlist the help of other family members and friends to send the notes or make the phone calls, especially when the wedding is canceled and it is extremely painful for the bride. If the bride wishes to keep the reason for the cancellation private, she instructs her mother and any close friends and relatives to not discuss the reasons why with the guests being notified. The guests, should not ask for an explanation unless the bride willingly offers one. If a guest is insensitive enough to ask, she may decline to answer graciously or simply say something like, "My reasons are private; thank you for your concern."

Cancellation

If a wedding is canceled, it is proper for you to return all wedding and engagement presents. Since the gifts are usually sent to the bride's house, sending the gifts back becomes her responsibility. If a gift was monogrammed, it can be kept.

Otherwise, the gifts should be mailed or delivered back to the sender, tagged with a brief note that reads something like:

Dear Jim and Marti,
Since my wedding has been cancelled, I am returning the beautiful candlesticks you so kindly sent me. Thank you for your thoughtfulness. Hope you are well.

Sincerely,
Mary Kay

Death in the Family

If someone in the immediate family of either the bride or groom dies shortly before the wedding, the wedding can be postponed; or, it can be scaled down to a modest gathering of close family members. If the latter is decided, invitation recalls should be sent to the guests.

An example of how to word the card is below:

Mr. and Mrs. Paul Dickson
regret that
due to a death in the family
the invitations
to their daughter's wedding
on the thirteenth of June,
must be recalled

After the wedding, announcements should be sent to everyone who receives such a recall. The bride should try to return all gifts under these circumstances, albeit some guests will insist that the couple keeps them. If a guest insists you keep his or her wedding gift, graciously accept it and write a thank-you note immediately.

Postponement

If the wedding is postponed and a date is set, the bride should keep all gifts. This is true even if the wedding is changed to a much later date. Of course, the guest is expected to give the couple a wedding gift only once.

Service Professionals

Your wedding's service providers, from the musicians to the caterers, typically have contracts explaining their policies should a need to cancel or postpone arise. You will need to contact each of those people as well—the sooner, the better. If the wedding is postponed, some vendors might reschedule (their schedule permitting) for no charge, but some vendors have nonrefundable retainers. Also, you can usually count on losing any deposits that have been made. You should also notify the newspapers that the wedding is either canceled or postponed.

470

Chapter Fourteen: The Honeymoon and Beyond

Time to Open Presents

Opening wedding presents is like peering into your future as husband and wife. It is fun to imagine using new pots and pans, silverware, and towels. If you can open your presents with close friends and family soon after the wedding or honeymoon, that usually works the best. After all, it is fun for them to see what you have received.

Usually, a bridesmaid or girlfriend of the bride makes a list of gifts and the names of the givers. It is imperative that whomever writes this list does so accurately and legibly.

The only gift is a portion of thyself.
— Ralph Waldo Emerson

Damaged Gifts

If a present is broken upon being opened, the bride and groom can return it to the store where it was purchased and explain what happened to the store manager. There is no need to tell the giver. Usually, the store (especially if it is one where the couple registered) will happily exchange or refund the money spent on the gift. If the gift was mailed, it is permissible to tell the giver so he or she can obtain reimbursement from insurance.

Thank-you Cards

You are starting a new life, and this new life might transplant you to a new house, apartment, state, or country. The last thing you want to do (or have time to do) is to write hundreds of thank-you notes. However, there is no getting around it. It is very poor etiquette not to send a personal, handwritten thank-you note to each person or family who sent a wedding gift. If possible, try to have the notes mailed within a month or two of the wedding date, and the sooner the better.

In past years, it was the sole responsibility of the bride to write each and every thank-you note. Recently, however, it has become perfectly acceptable for the groom to lend a hand. The task can be divided several ways. For example, the groom writes thank-you notes for gifts received from his friends and family, and the bride writes notes for the gifts received from her friends and family.

If getting the thank-you cards mailed within three months of your wedding is impossible for extremely busy newlyweds, they might have preprinted gift acknowledgments mailed to their giftgiving guests.

The acknowledgment reads something similar to:

> *Mr. and Mrs. Harold Jarvis*
> *wish to acknowledge the receipt*
> *of your wedding gift*
> *and will write you a personal note*
> *as soon as possible*

Of course, the acknowledgment does not relinquish the need for a personal thank-you note. It merely allows the newlyweds additional time in getting the cards written and mailed.

Do not send thank-you messages for wedding gifts via e-mail, and do not send a typed, vague form-letter or preprinted card. A handwritten, thank-you letter on the bride's personal stationery is the most acceptable way to show your appreciation. If her stationery is monogrammed, she should use the name she wants to be called after the wedding.

If you wish to send matching thank-you notes, these can be purchased with the wedding invitations so they coordinate. Some have the couple's monogram embossed on the front, or some simply state: "Thank You" on the front. Perhaps your photography package includes note cards with a place for one of your formal wedding photographs. Any of these are fine, as long as a personal, handwritten message is added.

What you write inside the card is up to you; however, here are some tips:

• Use the person's first name if you are close. (Dear Mary and Jon)

- Use the person's surname if you are more formally acquainted. (Dear Mr. and Mrs. White)
- Mention the gift in detail, even if it is money. (Thank you for the green and red holiday towel sets.) (Thank you for the check for fifty dollars.)
- Explain what you are going to do with the gift, or make something up if you are not sure. (The clock looks so grand in our hallway.) (We will be putting your money toward a new couch for the living room.)
- If the person came to the wedding, let him or her know you appreciated seeing them there. (It was so nice for you to travel such a great distance to share our special day with us!)
- If the person could not come due to illness, wish him or her well. (We missed you and hope you are feeling better.)

- Add any other information to give the note a personal touch. (Your friendship means the world to us.)
- Sign it as a couple. (Jason and Kim) (Mr. and Mrs. Ryan O'Dell)

Also, keep in mind that regardless of how you view a gift, it is important to send a sincere thank you. You do not necessarily have to lie; just use blanket adjectives such as "sweet," "thoughtful," and "unique."

Honeymoon

Long ago, as the story goes, a man grabbed a woman he was attracted to, and they hid in a place her loved ones would not discover. They stayed and drank a concoction made with honey until the moon went through all of its phases (about a month). This is where the word "honeymoon" came from. Today, however, a honeymoon is a vacation in which the newlyweds relax after the hubbub of the wedding and spend time cherishing and getting better acquainted with one another.

Traditionally, the groom and/or his parents pay for the entire honeymoon. Also, it is traditional for the newlyweds to leave on their honeymoon as soon after the reception as possible.

Some couples stay close to home, visiting a local resort. Others go on a romantic cruise to an exotic

479

island or a country half a world away. Some couples honeymoon for a long weekend, and others go for months. If a couple cannot afford the honeymoon of their dreams, or if they cannot miss work immediately after the wedding, they can plan a honeymoon for a later date.

Ideally, a honeymoon is a time free of work matters, the needs of other family members, and other everyday occurrences. However, sometimes a couple feels it important to include their parents or their children in their honeymoon plans. If others join you on your honeymoon, do not share rooms and do arrange a portion of the time for just the two of you. Likewise, if you absolutely have to keep connected to the workplace via cellular phone or laptop during your honeymoon, try to spend as little time as possible tending to work matters.

Sex and Marriage

Whether or not to have sex before one is married is an ongoing controversy. With widespread sexually transmitted diseases (STDs), emotional detachment issues, unwanted pregnancy, and other circumstances, having sexual encounters can prove detrimental, dangerous, and even deadly. Most parents (and churches) cross their fingers that their children will wait until their wedding night to have sex. Ideally, no one will ever have sex with anyone other than his or her spouse, and this will form a rock-solid physical union between husband and wife. Many people would like to say, "I waited until my wedding night," and hear it said by their new spouse in return. Some cultures will not allow a woman to marry if she has already experienced sexual intercourse, and some religions do not allow a man or woman who has had sex to marry in their temples (sometimes indefinitely; sometimes it is permissible at a later time).

On the flip side, many feel that sex is paradoxically a source of fulfillment and trouble in any given marital relationship. Therefore, sex (in general, and/or with a future spouse) should be experienced and explored well before the wedding night. They can learn certain techniques from sexual partners, passing that knowledge and those skills to the marriage bed. Also, having sex with their intended before the wedding will bring up any incapability issues that can be eliminated for the betterment of the overall relationship. A man and woman's desire for one another ebbs and flows throughout their relationship, as they become more familiar with each other and their own bodies, as they age and mature, and as they experience life. A proponent of premarital (safe) sex would argue that sex is such an important part of marriage that it can ultimately (whether singled-out or grouped with other issues) determine whether a marriage succeeds or fails.

Whichever view on sex before marriage is taken, one thing is certain—this is a highly personal issue. Discussions of these matters should be primarily limited to one's partner. While parents and close friends may offer views and/or opinions in general terms, care must be taken not to reveal an intimate trust. As the old saying goes, "a gentleman (or lady) does not kiss and tell."

Drinking when we are not thirsty and making love at all seasons, madam: that is all there is to distinguish us from other animals.

— Pierre-Augustin de Beaumarchais

The Expectant Bride

When a couple becomes pregnant, they might decide to marry, especially if they were planning on marrying someday anyway. It is a widely held view that raising a child together is easier than raising a child as a single parent. When a couple is in love and has been together long enough to see their futures together, this can be a good idea. However, if the couple is getting married only because of the unplanned pregnancy, the likelihood of the marriage succeeding is doubtful. The welfare of the unborn child should be the top priority.

Wedding gowns for expectant brides can be purchased from many bridal boutiques. Or, a seamstress can make a special wedding gown. The bride should not drink champagne or any other alcoholic beverage at the reception. Other than that, if your significant other or you are the expectant bride, a wedding need not be any different than if there were no baby involved.

Sometimes, a family is embarrassed by the situation, thinking the guests will see you as immoral and them as unfit parents, and other such nonsense. If their feelings are such and you decide to have a smaller, intimate wedding with just the closest of friends and immediate family, this is highly acceptable and commendable.

Living Together First

Today, many couples live together before they marry. Some choose to live together to "test" the relationship, bringing each other's bad habits and quirks out into the open. Living together also brings out each other's skills, such as cooking, financial planning, decorating, etc.

Sexual compatibility can be more thoroughly explored when sharing the same bed. If all goes well after several months or a year or more, the couple might feel more comfortable with the marriage commitment. When a couple lives together and things go smoothly, friends and family might pressure them to marry.

If a couple who has been living together decides to get married, this is a wonderful occasion indeed, and it should be celebrated no differently than if they both still lived with their parents.

Marriage is more than four bare legs in a bed.
— Hoshang N. Akhtar

If You Wait for the Wedding Night

Sometimes, a man and woman marry without enjoying each other intimately beforehand. If either your new spouse or you have sexual experience, that person might want to ease the other into the process. If neither the man nor woman has ever had sex, consummating the marriage can be wonderful or terrible, depending largely on the preconceived notions about what sex should be like.

Occasionally, a couple's chemistry is such that a steamy love scene in the most romantic movie cannot do it justice. But more often, the couple feels so tired and overwhelmed by the wedding itself—not to mention the pressures of having sex right then and there—that they simply go through the motions. Keep in mind that you have your entire honeymoon—not to mention your whole lives—to work on fulfilling your spouse and yourself sexually.

If the eve of your wedding is your first sexual confrontation with your mate, you will need to discuss and decide which method (if any) of birth control you will use. Most childless couples want to be married for a while before starting a family. However, there are quite a few "honeymoon babies" born to many unprepared couples. If you decide to use birth control, it is best to be prepared with your choice of method before the wedding night. The bride and groom will want to have discussed and agreed upon this vital issue well before the wedding night.

The key to a successful marriage relationship is communication, and this is very true for your sexual relationship as well.

Find the person who will love you because of your differences and not in spite of them, and you have found a lover for life.
— Leo Buscaglia

What's Your Name?

In the past, a wife almost always took her husband's last name as soon as they wed. Today, however, many women do not. With strong footholds on their identities and careers, women sometimes keep their maiden names or opt for a combination of the two last names.

If the wife is taking the husband's last name, which most women continue to do, she will need to change her name on legal documents, including: her driver's license, passport, social security card, credit cards, ownership titles, insurance policies, financial plans, employment records, e-mail address, and checking account. Keep in mind that all signatures, monogrammed stationery, etc., before the wedding should be in the woman's maiden name. She does not use her husband's surname until after the wedding occurs. If Angela Black is a career woman who wishes to announce to her colleagues that her surname is different now that she married Fred White, she can send a note to her associates stating:

> *Ms. Angela Black*
> *has adopted the surname of White*
> *for all professional and social purposes.*

If the bride chooses to keep her maiden name, just the way it has always been, she need not make any changes to legal documents. Some people might find this odd and ask questions, but you have the right to be called your maiden name if that is what you want. For professional-career women who are known by their maiden or former married name—particularly for authors, politicians, actors, performers, and the like—keeping that name may be politically and financially imperative. You might want to take your marriage certificate along whenever you are in a situation that you need to prove that you are married.

Some women wish to hold onto their maiden name, while adding their married name. This can be done in a couple of ways. First, she can simply have her maiden surname follow her first name, which is followed by her married surname. For example, if Isabella Rodriguez marries Chester Anderson, she can be called Isabella Rodriguez Anderson. Another way to integrate both a woman's maiden name and married name is by hyphenating the two last names. For instance, the woman in the preceding example would be called Isabella Rodriguez-Anderson. Hyphenating the two last names is quickly gaining popularity. Very rarely, a man will take on his new wife's maiden name in conjunction with his own. For example, Jackson Sheen, who just married Stephanie Clayton, would be called Jackson Clayton-Sheen. Usually, the wife would take on the same format. So, if the couple decides on Clayton-Sheen, they both are called Clayton-Sheen, and so their children will be named.

It is beneficial to discuss what name you wish to be called well before the wedding. Sometimes, there are strong feelings about both options, and these feelings need to be explored. A compromise can be reached. Whichever name the wife (and husband) decides to use after marriage, it is just fine. For ease and to alleviate widespread confusion, it is recommended to make any name format changes immediately after the wedding on the mailed wedding announcements. Include notification to driver's license bureau and Social Security offices.

New Address

If the bride and groom have an address change after they marry, the addresses will need to be changed on their driver's licenses, checking accounts, and so forth. Both the bride and groom should fill out change-of-address forms at the post office, as well. If "At Home" cards (see page 270) were not sent out to friends and family by now, "We Have Moved" cards can be mailed to those people who would like to know your new address. It is also acceptable to e-mail the new address information to people.

Another Big Day

Here is a small piece of advice that will help keep your marriage forever happy: Do not forget your wedding anniversary! Never! Even if times are rough, do anything you can think of to make your spouse feel special and loved, especially on your anniversary.

Following is a list of traditional and contemporary wedding anniversary gifts. While people today rarely adhere to these themes, this list can help.

Wedding Anniversary Gifts

	Traditional	*Contemporary*
First Year	Paper	Clock
Second Year	Cotton	China
Third Year	Leather	Crystal
Fourth Year	Linen	Electrical Appliance
Fifth Year	Wood	Silverware
Sixth Year	Iron	Wood
Seventh Year	Wool or Copper	Desk Set
Eighth Year	Bronze	Linen
Ninth Year	Pottery	Leather
Tenth Year	Tin or Aluminum	Diamond
Eleventh Year	Steel	Jewelry
Twelfth Year	Silk	Pearl

Thirteenth Year	Lace	Fur
Fourteenth Year	Ivory	Gold
Fifteenth Year	Crystal or Glass	Watch
Twentieth Year	China	Platinum
Twenty-fifth Year	Silver	Sterling Silver
Thirtieth Year	Pearl	Diamond
Thirty-fifth Year	Coral or Jade	Jade
Fortieth Year	Ruby	Ruby
Forty-fifth Year	Sapphire	Sapphire
Fiftieth Year	Gold	Gold
Fifty-fifth Year	Emerald	Emerald
Sixtieth Year	Diamond	Diamond

Reaffirming Your Vows

The reasons for a couple reaffirming their vows can be manifold; however the most prevalent include:

- It is a special anniversary, like the tenth, twenty-fifth or fiftieth.

- The couple did not have the wedding ceremony of their dreams and they want one now.
- The couple suffered a rocky period and wants to begin again, making a public profession of love and respect.
- The marriage is a second one and reaching a decade mark or more together feels as monumental as a twenty-fifth does to a traditional couple.

The ceremony usually takes place in the couple's or a special friend or relative's home, and it is similar to a wedding. Exchanging the vows is the main event, and usually a party takes place afterward.

To laugh often and love much . . . to appreciate beauty, to find the best in others, to give one's self . . . this is to have succeeded.

— Ralph Waldo Emerson

Bibliography

Ayers, Tess and Paul Brown, *The Essential Guide to Lesbian and Gay Weddings*, Alyson Books, Los Angeles, CA, 1999.

Beilenson, Esther Budoff, *I Do, I Do*, Peter Pauper Press, Inc., New York, 1991.

Dresser, Norine, *Multicultural Celebrations: Today's Rules of Etiquette for Life's Special Occasions*, Three Rivers Press, New York, 1999.

Gilbert, Edith, *The Complete Wedding Planner*, Warner Books, New York, 1983.

Griffin, Dinah Braun and Marla Schram Schwartz, *The Bride Guide*, Barricade Books Inc., New York, 1991.

Packham, Jo, *Wedding Ceremonies: Planning Your Special Day*, Sterling Publishing Co., Inc., New York, 1993.

Packham, Jo, *Wedding Gowns and Other Bridal Apparel*, Sterling Publishing Co., Inc., New York, 1994.

Post, Elizabeth L., *Emily Post's Complete Book of Wedding Etiquette*, Harper Collins Publishers, New York, 1991.

Post, Elizabeth L., *Emily Post on Weddings*, HarperPerennial, New York, 1987.

Stewart, Marjabelle Young, *The New Etiquette: Real Manners for Real People in Real Situations*, St. Martin's Press, Inc., New York.

Tober, Barbara, *The Bride: A Celebration*, Longmeadow Press, Stamford, Conneticut, 1984.

Photo Credits

Anthony Lordemann 216

Chapelle, Ltd. 172, 185, 477

Corbis Images (©1998) 200, 229, 232

Kim Taylor 78

PhotoDisc, Inc. Images (©1992, 1994, 1999, 2000) 9–10, 16, 22,

35, 38, 52, 62, 66, 71, 74, 98, 120, 131, 171, 175, 181, 194, 204, 233, 278, 284, 289, 298, 309, 319, 322, 328, 338, 350, 357, 358, 365, 369, 377–378, 387, 393, 396, 399, 406, 412, 423, 426, 430, 437, 441–442, 462, 468, 470, 479

Scherry Tibbins Moore 148, 167

INDEX

500

If you liked this book, you'll love this series:

Little Giant Encyclopedia of Aromatherapy • Little Giant Encyclopedia of Baseball Quizzes • Little Giant Encyclopedia of Card & Magic Tricks • Little Giant Encyclopedia of Card Games • Little Giant Encyclopedia of Card Games Gift Set • Little Giant Encyclopedia of Checker Puzzles • Little Giant Encyclopedia of Dream Symbols •Little Giant Encyclopedia of Etiquette • Little Giant Encyclopedia of Feng Shui • Little Giant Encyclopedia of Fortune Telling • Little Giant Encyclopedia of Handwriting Analysis • Little Giant Encyclopedia of IQ Tests • Little Giant Encyclopedia of Logic Puzzles • Little Giant Encyclopedia of Lucky Numbers • Little Giant Encyclopedia of Meditations & Blessings • Little Giant Encyclopedia of Mensa Mind-Teasers • Little Giant Encyclopedia of One-Liners • Little Giant Encyclopedia of Palmistry • Little Giant Encyclopedia of Proverbs • Little Giant Encyclopedia of Puzzles • Little Giant Encyclopedia of Runes • Little Giant Encyclopedia of Spells & Magic • Little Giant Encyclopedia of Superstitions • Little Giant Encyclopedia of Toasts & Quotes • Little Giant Encyclopedia of Wedding Toasts • Little Giant Encyclopedia of Wedding Etiquette • Little Giant Encyclopedia of the Zodiac

Available at fine stores everywhere.